Routledge Revivals

Socialism and the Market

ECONOMIC PLANNING IN SOVIET RUSSIA

By

BORIS BRUTZKUS

With a Foreword by

F. A. HAYEK

ROUTLEDGE REVIVALS
Routledge
Taylor & Francis Group

First published in 1935 by George Routledge & Sons Ltd

This edition first published in 2018 by Routledge
2 Park Square, Milton Park, Abingdon, Oxon, OX14 4RN
and by Routledge
711 Third Avenue, New York, NY 10017

Routledge is an imprint of the Taylor & Francis Group, an informa business

Publisher's Note
The publisher has gone to great lengths to ensure the quality of this reprint but points out that some imperfections in the original copies may be apparent.

Disclaimer
The publisher has made every effort to trace copyright holders and welcomes correspondence from those they have been unable to contact.
A Library of Congress record exists under ISBN: 35003617

ISBN 13: 978-1-138-55827-4 (hbk)
ISBN 13: 978-1-138-56608-8 (pbk)
ISBN 13: 978-1-315-12333-2 (ebk)

Socialism and the Market

Socialism and the Market

The Socialist Calculation Debate Revisited

Volume III

Selected by Peter J. Boettke

Economic Planning in Soviet Russia

Boris Brutzkus

London and New York

First published 1935 by George Routledge & Sons Ltd
This edition reprinted 2000
by Routledge
11 New Fetter Lane, London EC4P 4EE

Simultaneously published in the USA and Canada
by Routledge
29 West 35th Street, New York, NY 10001

Routledge is an imprint of the Taylor & Francis Group

Typeset by Graphicraft Ltd, Hong Kong
Printed and bound in Great Britain by TJI Digital, Padstow, Cornwall

British Library Cataloguing in Publication Data
A catalogue record for this book is available from the British Library

Library of Congress Cataloging in Publication Data
A catalogue record for this book has been requested

ISBN 0-415-19586-1 (set)
ISBN 0-415-19589-6 (Volume III)

Publisher's note

The publisher has gone to great lengths to ensure the quality of these reprints, but wishes to point out that certain characteristics of the originals will, of necessity, be apparent thereof.

ECONOMIC PLANNING IN SOVIET RUSSIA

By

BORIS BRUTZKUS

With a Foreword by

F. A. HAYEK

LONDON

GEORGE ROUTLEDGE & SONS, LTD.

BROADWAY HOUSE: 68–74 CARTER LANE, E.C.

1935

Translated from the
German by
GILBERT GARDINER

CONTENTS

CONTENTS

FOREWORD

It can hardly be said that the intense interest with which, for more than fifteen years, all the world has been watching the developments in Russia has been rewarded with an amount of instruction at all commensurate with the space it has occupied among the topics of general discussion. Few of those who have been following the ever-increasing stream of literature on the subject can have felt satisfied that they ever really knew what was happening in that country and a great many have by now practically abandoned the attempt to form a clear opinion of the results so far achieved. It is fashionable to speak of it as the great experiment and to emphasize its importance for the future of the human race, but how many who use these phrases really know what the whole thing actually means.

To some degree this unsatisfactory state of affairs is due to the political passions involved which inevitably deprive much of the available information of reliability. But this cannot fully account for the existing situation. During the last few years there has certainly been no lack of dispassionate attempts at a serious examination of the problem, and yet in most cases the outcome has been singularly inconclusive. About the central problem, the advantages or disadvantages of centralized economic planning, the difficulties which the Soviet Government has met and the degree to which it has solved them, our knowledge has not much increased. The reason for this is the extraordinary scarcity of information on which conclusions of this sort could be based. The difficulties which have to be overcome in this respect are so immense that only an investigator of quite exceptional qualifications could hope to overcome them.

But among those who have been attracted to such investigations, the majority have lacked even the first requisite for really successful researches—mastery of the Russian language. Where most of the really relevant information has to be laboriously collected from occasional statements in internal Russian discussions, and where all information made available in foreign language is notoriously misleading, it is impossible for anyone who does not possess a full command of the language to hope to get very far. But a qualification no less important but much more rare is such an intimate knowledge of the country, its history and institutions, and of the psychology of its people, as will enable the observer to separate what is specifically Russian and independent of the system by which that country is at present governed, from the consequences which can be said properly to derive from the existing system. It is not really surprising that most of the accounts of modern Russia hardly penetrate at all below the surface. No doubt as the impressions of intelligent men they have a certain interest. But they certainly contain little answer to the main question.

But beyond this there is a further qualification necessary. Even the most careful study of the Russian facts cannot lead very far if it is not guided by a clear conception of what the problem is; i.e. if it is not undertaken by a person who, before he embarks on the investigations of the special problems of Russia, has arrived at a clear idea of the fundamental task that economic planning involves.

It is improbable that anyone but a Russian economist will ever combine the qualifications required for the successful conduct of such a study. But the number of Russian economists who still really know their country and who at the same time are in the position to speak freely about the present events has become very limited. Among those who remain the author of the present volume may claim to speak with special authority. Professor of agricultural economics at Petersburg from 1907 to 1922 and long recognized as one of the first authorities on Russian agriculture, Professor Brutzkus has followed the developments with an active interest at close quarters. In his book on the *Agricultural Development and Agricultural Revolution in Russia* [1] he has given us a most illuminating and certainly not unsympathetic account of the trends that led to the Revolution. From the very beginning of the new regime he devoted himself to an intense study of the tasks it had set itself, and as early as 1920 he produced, under circumstances which he describes in his preface, the remarkable survey of the economic problems raised by socialism, which in a slightly abridged English translation forms now the first part of the present volume. If one reads it to-day, in the light of the developments that have since taken place in Russia and of the extensive discussions

[1] This work was published in German. Its original title is *Agrarentwicklung und Agrarrevolution in Russland.* Mit einem Vorwort von Max Sering ("Quellen und Studien" herausagegeben vom Osteuropa-Institut in Breslau, Abt. Wirtschaft) Berlin, 1926.

which have been devoted to the problem of collectivist planning,[1] one is still struck by the extraordinary clarity with which at that early date its author had grasped the really central problems. Together with the works of Professor L. Mises and Max Weber, which appeared in Germany only a few months earlier, this book must indeed be regarded as one of the chief of those studies which initiated the modern discussion of the economic problems of socialism.

This critical analysis of the problems of socialism assumes special significance from the fact that it deals not only with socialism in general, but also with the concrete problems of a country which for more than a dozen years has actually had to try to solve the problems. The attentive reader who keeps in mind the date when it was written will again and again be struck by the extraordinary foresight shown by the author and the degree to which his predictions have been verified by actual events. Not only the more spectacular changes of economic policy which have occurred during the period but also many of the minor events in the history of the Russian experiment are clearly foreshadowed in his discussion. This is clearly demonstrated in the second part of the volume where the developments of the past fifteen years are analysed.

For some time after the publication of this criticism Professor Brutzkus was still allowed to remain in the country, and for a time in 1922 he even acted as chairman

[1] An account of these discussions together with a collection of translations of the more important critical studies of the economic problems of socialism by continental writers will appear simultaneously with the present book in a companion volume under the title *Collectivist Economic Planning*, edited by F. A. Hayek.

of the agricultural planning commission for the Petrograd district in the people's commissariat for agriculture. But at the end of that year he was compelled to leave the country and settled in Germany where, for a period of ten years, he was Professor at the Russian Scientific Institute at Berlin, a position which he lost after the National Socialist Revolution. This position enabled him, however, to follow events in Russia closely and to study all aspects of the further economic developments of that country in great detail. Numerous publications (mostly in German) which appeared during the course of this period bear witness to the uninterrupted attention which he devoted to every phase of that phenomenon. A short study reviewing the results of the First Five Year Plan, which appeared in 1932, has attracted particularly wide attention.[1] In the second part of the present volume he has now elaborated this into a more comprehensive survey of economic planning in Russia from the revolution to the present time. It seems to me that in it he has succeeded in throwing more light on the history of this experiment than any other work known to me. His familiarity with the Russian scene has enabled him to draw on relatively inaccessible sources which, just because they were not prepared for foreign consumption, tell more about the actual situation than volumes of official statistics. Yet, as the reader will notice, the fragments of information from which he pieces together his surprisingly complete and illuminating picture are all gathered from statements from the most authoritative sources. I do not hesitate to place his work as it is now collected in the present volume in

[1] *Der Fünfjahresplan und seine Erfüllung*, Leipzig, Verlag Deutsche Wissenschaftliche Buchhandlung, 1932.

the very first rank of the really scientific literature on present-day Russia. It is to be hoped that in its English form it will have the same success as its German predecessors.

F. A. HAYEK.

London School of Economics and Political Science.
October 1934.

PART I

THE DOCTRINES OF MARXISM IN THE LIGHT OF THE RUSSIAN REVOLUTION

(1920)

PREFACE

THE ideas set forth in these pages matured in my mind during the early years of constructive communism in Petrograd. I was first given the opportunity of enlarging upon them in August 1920, when I lectured to an academic audience in that city. The communist government, intoxicated by its successes in the counter-revolution, had promised to deal promptly with all economic problems now that its hands were free to do so. It was at this moment of its greatest triumphs that I put forward my contention that the system of Marxian communism, as then conceived, was—quite apart from the conditions produced by the war—intrinsically unsound and must inevitably break down. My lecture aroused much interest, and I repeated it several times in private.

Before long the retreat of communism had set in. In March 1921, Lenin had no choice but to announce the New Economic Policy (N.E.P.), which entailed the rejection of " natural socialism " and the reconstruction of an economy based on money.

There seemed to be some hope just then of a revival of non-communist literature. Certain private firms in Petrograd showed signs of great activity and, what was more, a few non-communist newspapers were permitted to appear. I therefore decided to have my articles on socialism printed in the *Economist*, a journal which the Russian Technical Society had been publishing since the end of 1921, under the title, " The Problems of National

Economy under the Socialist Order." I hoped that the spell of Marxism might now be broken, after the bitter experiences undergone by the communists, and that a contemporary Russian criticism of socialism might prove interesting at this juncture. And this time my faith in the tolerance of the communists was justified. My treatise ran through three numbers of the journal and only a few controversial paragraphs were suppressed by the censor.

But, alas, this " lucid interval " of tolerance was of short duration. By the summer of 1922 the censorship had been tightened, and after the double number IV–V of the *Economist* appeared, further publication was forbidden and the existing copies were seized from the bookshops. When the communist congress met in August of that year, Sinoviev proclaimed a spiritual war against the bourgeois ideology. Act I of this " spiritual war " consisted in mass arrests of Intellectuals in Moscow and Petrograd. Early on the morning of August 17th, 1922, a large portion of the editorial staff of the *Economist*, including the present writer, were lodged in the notorious prison of the former Cheka in the Gorochovaya Street.

These prisoners had nothing to do with politics as such. They were professors—of philosophy, jurisprudence, economics, even higher mathematics—or well-known publicists and literary men who had hardly had a chance of publishing anything for four years back. But to be non-political is no protection against violence in a communist state, where not only deeds, but opinions can be regarded as criminal. Still, the communist rulers behaved with unusual leniency on this occasion, for we were merely ordered to quit the country with all possible haste. Trotsky, who at that time played the leading part in political life, described the Soviet Government's attitude towards us as " preventive humanity ". He little knew that the same fate was to overtake him a few years later. " Learned ideologists ", he wrote in the *Pravda*, " are not at present dangerous to the Republic, but external or internal complications might arise which would oblige us to have these ideologists shot. Better let them go abroad therefore." The German Government responded very kindly to our request for visas and we were thus enabled to conform to the Soviet's orders.

In publishing in a foreign country the essays which I wrote on socialism at that time, I have thought it right to refrain from any alterations or additions based on the more recent literature on this subject ; for this could only spoil the character of a criticism of socialism that is unique in that, by chance, it was published under Soviet rule.[1]

Since the transition to the N.E.P., Soviet Russia has shelved for the time being the idea of natural socialism. But the system has not been definitely overthrown in that country and still less is this the case in other countries, where socialism is still thought of as a system with a no-money basis. I therefore feel entitled to express my confidence that this brief essay, written under the direct impression of the tremendous Russian upheaval and consisting of a criticism of natural socialism and the economic theories of Marxism bound up with it, will be found to have retained its actuality in the English version.

[1] All I have permitted myself is the insertion of certain passages suppressed by the censor and the addition of a final paragraph, which though a logical sequel to the whole could not have been printed in Russia.

I

MARXISM AND THE PROBLEM OF SOCIALIST ECONOMICS

It is customary to divide the history of the development of socialist doctrine into two periods: the period of Utopian, and the period of scientific, socialism. Such a division is crude, as it is possible to discover scientific elements in the so-called Utopian socialism and unscientific elements in the so-called scientific socialism; yet in principle it is right. The division between the two periods is formed by the works of the greatest of socialist thinkers and politicians, Karl Marx. Taking the idea of evolution as his starting-point, Marx sought in this way to interpret the events of social economic development. The method proved as fruitful in the social sciences as in all other spheres of scientific thought. In the second half of the past century Marxism won for itself a position of absolute domination within the socialist movement, and even to-day it remains the dogma of the revolutionary proletariat. In the same way it is the basis of the Russian communist party's programme.

The Utopian socialists believed that the socialist order would come into being through the initiative of small social groups which, convinced as to the benefits to be derived from socialism, would carry the rest of society with them in the fervency of their belief. In contradiction to this conception of the evolution of social phenomena, Marx maintained that social economic events must result from the action of the elemental processes of nature. The objective investigation of capitalist evolution leads, according to Marx, to the irrefutable conclusion that capitalism is marching inexorably towards its own fall, and that in its womb the elements of a new social order—the socialist order—are ripening. Thus Marx held that the immediate task of his age was not the establishing of small social groups on a socialist foundation, but in the consolidation and organisation of the proletariat as a class ; a class whose task should be, at a given point in social economic evolution—i.e. at the moment when the final crisis was upon capitalism—to take upon itself the reconstruction of society as a whole, and to rebuild it on a socialist foundation.

But in this way the essential substance of socialist doctrine was transformed. While the Utopian socialists stressed the task of building up a new society, scientific socialism concentrated most of its attention upon a criticism of the existing economic system, and upon the explanation of the evolution of this system. It is true that this evolution was supposed to prescribe certain basic principles for the coming socialist society, but with the systematic construction of such a society Marx did not concern himself.

No more did the followers of Marx devote themselves to this problem. Even that versatile and exceptionally productive writer, Karl Kautsky, whose work in the investigation of social economic processes with the help of the methods of Marxism was so notable, remained unfruitful in this field.

The socialist revolution which was consummated in

Russia seems at last to have confronted orthodox Russian socialists with the task of constructing socialism in the form of a positive doctrine. But even Russian socialist literature of the time was unable to render any service in this direction. In his *Economics of the Transition period* N. Bucharin, the prominent Bolshevist theoretician, contents himself with affirming the old socialist proposition that the categories of the capitalist economic system would lose their significance under socialism. He makes no attempt to explain what categories would regulate production and consumption under the new economic system. It is true that there exists in Russian literature an attempt to construct socialism as a positive doctrine, but this attempt was undertaken by the late M. J. Tugan-Baranovsky, who, of course, cannot be described as an orthodox Marxist. Thus the bewildering but indubitable fact remains : *Scientific socialism, confining itself exclusively to a criticism of the capitalist economic order, has so far produced no theory for a socialist economic order.*

And yet there was no adequate reason why Marxism should refrain from propounding such a theory. For although Marx made the evolutionary method the cardinal point in his system of thought, he never ceased on that account to be a revolutionary. In the famous dispute between Lenin and Kautsky as to whether Marx conceived the transformation of capitalist into socialist society as a gradual process, made up of a series of partial reforms (as Kautsky maintains) or whether he foresaw a simultaneous revolution (as Lenin believes)—in this dispute we must give the verdict decisively in favour of Lenin. Indeed, Kautsky, in his paper, *The Social Revolution*, has himself paid homage to the same view. Hegel's scheme of dialectic evolution which was recognised by Marx and according to which quantitative changes take place under the old forms—this scheme postulates revolutionary eruptions, in which qualitative changes of the social material take place as a result of the accumulated quantitative changes.

Marx frequently compared the origin of a new society with physiological birth. Let us adopt this analogy and attempt to draw from it its necessary conclusions. The child only comes into the world after all its organs have been developed within the body of its mother; yet birth is not altogether a mechanical act, for it involves a radical physiological transformation in the living body thus thrust upon the world. In order to be able to exist in its new environment the new-born child must be able to suck and breathe, two altogether new processes which are instinctive in origin. Now analogous phenomena must also be found in the case of the birth of a new social society. The entrepreneur in search of profit, who hitherto has set in motion the whole economic mechanism of society, disappears under the new system. New motives must appear in economic life. But—society is not an organism in the literal sense of the word, and it therefore lacks all directive instincts. The new processes, which arise instinctively in an organic being, must rather, if they are to occur in a social body, be considered beforehand by its leaders.

Now if capitalistic society, which leaves the satisfaction of its most important needs to the free initiative of its members, and which restricts the economic functions of the state to a certain regulation of the economic activities of individuals, if this social order has created the science of political economy, how much more indispensable is such a science to a socialist society in which the state takes upon itself an infinitely more responsible, various and complicated economic activity.

The fact that socialism as a creative doctrine within Marxism has hitherto remained undeveloped can only be explained by the suggestion that Marxists did not possess the courage to undertake the solution of a problem which had been left unsolved by Marx himself. For the fulfilment of the practical task which Marx regarded as of supreme importance,—i.e. for the organisation of a united international workers' movement,—a deeply penetrating study of the theory of socialist economics was in no respect absolutely necessary. On the contrary, in order to organise the proletariats for a war against capitalism, it was sufficient to throw a critical and searching light upon the darker aspects of the capitalist economic system, and to describe socialism, on the other hand, only in the most general and alluring terms. But after Marx's death, social economic evolution progressed without interruption, and the problem of social evolution and of the construction of a new social order became more and more real and pressing.

It was necessary to *prepare* for the execution of these undertakings and the fact that, when the time came, the Marxists were unprepared necessarily had consequences which were unfavourable to the socialist movement. At a time when, thanks to a world war of unprecedented destructive force, the economic life of the civilised nations appeared to be threatened with ruin, and capitalism was faced with a crisis such as it had never before experienced, the disadvantages of this failure on the part of socialist theory necessarily became clearly evident. The leaders of West European Socialism were quite unexpectedly called to power by the permanent opposition. As, however, they did not posesss a comprehensive plan for the construction of a new social order the old leaders of Western Socialism, fully conscious of their heavy responsibilities to the working class, did not dare to encourage the masses to bring about a social revolution. They are no longer convinced that socialism is capable, in the difficult circumstances which prevailed, of curing the ills of our time. Fearful lest they disorganise completely an economic system which is already in a state of confusion, they are timid—even in their proposals for reform. On the other hand, there are the all-powerful Russian socialists, who are undoubtedly more uncompromising in their devotion to the Marxian doctrine, and are by nature more daring and determined. They, with the social revolution already an accomplished fact, yet lacking any definite plan, to-day find themselves compelled to jump from one experiment to another ; and this at a time when, in view of the extremely critical economic situation, they should proceed with the utmost possible assurance.

If, now, we consider all these serious negative effects, resulting from the lack of a socialist economic theory which has been systematically elaborated for the needs of a socialist community, then we cannot avoid the conclusion that this lack is no accidental matter. The reasons for so serious a deficiency must be deeper. They will be disclosed as our exposition proceeds.

Although Marxism has produced no systematic theory for a socialist economy, it has nevertheless determined its outline. This follows partly as a consequence of the fact that socialism must originate in the transformation of capitalism, and partly because the social class which is to put socialism into effect is the industrial proletariat.

This general outline may be characterised as follows : Marxian socialism is not the socialism of small communities ; above all it is socialism in the grand manner, demanding the framework of a state and of a nation. Marxian socialism rejects in principle the market and market prices as regulating factors of production, so far as it concerns the distribution of the forces of production. These capitalistic methods of regulation are, from the Marxian point of view, untenable ; again and again Marxism emphasises the "anarchy of capitalist methods of production" which inevitably lead to periodical crises. It regards this anarchy as one of the greatest weaknesses of capitalism which socialism is called upon to overcome. In comparison with capitalism, socialism appears to be the most perfect form of economic organisation. Socialism directs the economic life according to a unitary state plan, which is founded upon statistics. Not only market prices, but also the other basic categories of the capitalist economy lose their significance under socialism. There are no wages, no profits and no rent, because in the socialist community everyone works and everyone receives the product of their work without the deduction of any forms of income which are not earned by active labour. The only form of production costs recognised by socialism are labour costs ; the measurement of such costs is based upon the time required for the work. Even in the capitalist society labour is the one and only force capable of creating value—such is the assertion of Marx in the first volume of *Das Kapital* ; all the more is this assertion applicable to the socialist economic order. In the socialist society the division of economic goods must be carried out in accordance with the principle of equality. As liberty is the guiding principle of the *bourgeoisie*, so equality is the watchword of the industrial proletariat. In the name of equality the great social revolution will be accomplished.

These then are the leading principles of Marxian socialism in regard to the construction of a new economic system. Whether it is possible to find a real solution to the problem of constructing theoretically a socialist economic order—this we shall disclose in the following pages. At any rate, any work devoted to this problem is of great significance for the better understanding of the capitalist system. While investigating the fundamental problems of socialist economics we may hope to throw light upon new aspects of the problems of capitalism.

II

SOCIALISM AND THE ECONOMIC PRINCIPLE

No economist would willingly dispute the correctness of the proposition that every economic activity—whether it be carried on within the framework of a natural, a capitalist or a socialist economy—must obey the principle that its results must correspond to the costs expended upon them. Not in vain is this principle deemed to be the essential characteristic of economic activity, distinguishing it from every other form of human activity. Only it is to be presumed that under socialism this principle would assume a peculiar form which is adapted to socialism.

The manner in which the economic principle is realised within the natural economy is obvious. A restricted group of individuals, bound together by ties of blood and common life, work and consume all goods produced by the group ; here there arises quite naturally a certain subjectively determined proportion between the costs, which consist chiefly of labour outlay, and the value of the products of this labour, which are consumed by the workers themselves as well as by their relatives. The limited range and complete distinctness of the whole production process in this case provides a certain guarantee that this proportion will be steadily maintained.

Under the capitalist system the entrepreneur makes use of the labour of strangers, with whose welfare he is not concerned ; he makes free use of material and machines which represent the products of earlier productive processes ; and he also utilises the forces of nature, to which he stands in quite a different relation than did the workers under the natural economy. Nevertheless, there also arises in the course of this much more complex economic process, a rational relationship between the cost and result of production, a relation which finds an even more consistent and distinct expression here than in the natural economy. All the elements of production—labour, fuel, machines, and the use of capital and land—attain a market value just as much as the products of production. This evaluation takes place by virtue of a spontaneous process, the results of which must be taken by the entrepreneur as data. Now if the price (market value) of his products does not cover the cost of producing them, the entrepreneur loses the power of disposing over the means of production, and he will be forced out of business, irresistibly and inexorably, as the elementary economic process takes its course. For he is unable to perform the task which society has assigned to him as entrepreneur, the task of so combining the elements of production that their cost is covered by the market price of the goods produced by means of them. On the other hand, capitalism rewards no one so generously, not even the great artist or scientist, as the skilful entrepreneur who is able to combine the elements of production successfully ; and this, though the needs which he satisfies be of the most prosaic order. Thus, in the capitalist society, the entrepreneur's condition is one of sustained exertion, and this he seeks to communicate to all who take part in production. Some he will endeavour to interest directly in the goods he has produced, others he will spur on by means of increased wages, others he will hold in check by threats of dismissal. Thus in the capitalist society, divided as it is into classes and separate groups of owners, the economic principle finds realisation.

How may the same principle be realised in a socialist society? In this form of society, unlike the capitalist, there is no great body of entrepreneurs whose economic standing gives them an interest in bringing about successful production. On the contrary, the managers of socialist enterprises gain nothing in material profit if the efforts of the management are successful, any more than they suffer if the results of such efforts are unfavourable. For it is not they who have to pay for the use of labour, of capital, and of natural resources in the process of production, no more do they win any sort of advantage from the goods supplied to society. In the case of every socialist management the risks are transferred from its members to society as a whole.

We do not propose to dwell further on the difficulties, of a subjective nature, which would be met with in the construction of a socialist society as a result of this psychological factor; for the investigation of the subjective elements of economic activity is fraught with difficulty, and the findings of such an investigation will always be disputed. We will content ourselves with the following objective conclusion, the truth of which has been clearly demonstrated by the foregoing remarks. *Economic calculation is of far greater significance in the socialist than in the capitalist society.* The capitalist entrepreneur may, if he likes, keep no books at all. So much the worse for him—he will make a gamble of his business. But his responsibility to the economic community is none the less for that, for society provides him with all his requirements at a definite price and in the same way buys from him at a definite price. "And he will not escape the judgment of the world."[1] If he wastes the forces of production he will pay for his folly with his fortune and his social position. Not so in the socialist society. If a large-scale concern is conducted without the assistance of proper calculation, its manager may nevertheless lead an untroubled life, however great may be the waste of society's means of production which is caused by the irrational organisation of the undertaking. Nevertheless, such a concern will be like a sick member of an economic organisation, and even if the disease is not discovered it will not be the less dangerous for that ; just as in the living organism a wound which causes no pain is not less dangerous. Thus there can be no greater peril to the socialist society than the atrophy of economic calculation, for this cannot but be followed by the disorganisation of the whole economic system.

It is precisely this atrophy of economic calculation which we have witnessed in Russia. It has taken place along with the precipitate growth of Socialism—at the expense of private property—while the market and money economy have perished. In the *Economics of the Transition Period*, which we have already cited, it is shown convincingly with the example of the railways that the old methods of cost calculation have lost all their significance to-day. This has clearly not caused the socialist theoretician any anxiety. Bucharin indeed recognises the need for some other system of making up accounts, but he does not give any detailed exposition of its principles. This, however, is precisely the weak point

[1] From Pushkin's *Boris Godunov*.

of our socialist economy. It is true that milk is produced, bread is baked, rolling-stock is repaired, and coal is transported; but no one is able to say how much these processes cost us. This state of affairs necessarily led the economic system towards catastrophe, and the catastrophe has come about.

Although the state no longer possessed the earlier means of cost calculation, it naturally could not forgo control over its enterprises. But it was only able to control separate factors of production. In this connection, however, its activities were necessarily very far-reaching, and considerably more so than those of the capitalists. It introduced a minute supervision of the superficial conduct of employees, of the consumption of materials, of machines and of stock. Revision after revision was instituted and there arose an abnormal disproportion between the producing and controlling mechanisms. And yet this system of control over the elements of production provided no guarantee as to the economic rationality of the process of production as a whole; nor did it possess that decisive significance which the calculation of costs possessed under capitalism. It may even be said—in spite of the moralists—that the managerial integrity which can best achieve such control is not in a position to assure the community against loss, while on the other hand a measure of dishonesty may not be without its economic uses. It all depends upon whether the organisation of production is successful or the reverse; and for this such control can provide no criterion.

And indeed we see to-day that the state has realised the impossibility of maintaining economic life in this manner. A way out was found in the restoration of the free market and in the calculation of the profitability of separate state undertakings, this calculation being based on data provided by the market. Such a method, however, does not lie within the framework of socialism as Marx conceived it, and what interests us is precisely the solution of the problem of economic calculation under Marxian socialism.

After establishing the atrophy of the old forms of economic calculation Bucharin asserts that calculation in kind should take its place. This idea was further developed by A. W. Tschajanow, who is of the opinion that the new method would make it possible to compare the separate undertakings in a socialist state according to the degree in which they were rationally organised. For example, in applying his method to agriculture, he makes this sort of calculation : the production of 1,000 units of grain requires the following expenditure : 30 units of labour, 90 units of the means of subsistence, 8·6 units of land, 0·2 units of transport, 25·6 units of buildings, 0·4 units of stock, 1·5 units of material, 0·03 units of heating. In order to arrive at this complex formula Tschajanow had to look for a common unit for all the means of subsistence, a common unit for all buildings, for all sorts of stock from harrows to steam threshing-machines, and for all sorts of material, from lubricating oil to string. Now it is clear that the value of all these units will be very hypothetical or entirely arbitrary. They will only have any real significance in so far as they are worked out on the basis of a common principle of value ; the author, however, did not succeed in doing this. Besides, if the director of the Russian agricultural estates only receives the balance sheets in the form described, he will not be able to do anything with them. If, however, the units of measure for buildings, means of subsistence, land and plant are to be brought to a common denominator, such a denominator will have to be defined.

It is no wonder that Tschajanow's attempt failed. S. Strumilin and E. Varga, who attacked the problem of economic calculation in *Ekonomitscheskaja Žizn'*[1] both rejected Tschajanow's method, and both came to the conclusion that, just as capitalism possessed a general measure of value in the rouble, so socialism would have to possess an analagous unit for the evaluation of its elements. Indeed, this conclusion is indisputable. *Without evaluation any rational economic conduct, under whatever kind of economic system, is impossible.* In full agreement with the basic principles of Marxism, Varga and Strumilin laid it down that labour would have to serve as the measure of value. Assuming that labour is, as Marx says, the real, if disguised, basis of the social evaluation of economic goods under capitalism and the basis of their exchange value, then labour must be all the more consciously made the basis of value under socialism.

In the following pages we shall therefore investigate the extent to which the measurement of value by labour can serve a socialist society. The problem is of the greatest theoretical interest, for it has an important bearing on the theoretical significance of the basic conceptions of Marxism with regard to economic activity.

[1] The leading economic paper in present-day Russia.

III

THE CALCULATION OF LABOUR VALUE IN THE SOCIALIST SOCIETY

LET us try to imagine, in concrete form, the calculation of the labour value of economic goods.

In our socialist state time appears as the measure of the quantity of labour. But even in a socialist society it is impossible to overlook so fundamental a characteristic of labour as its productivity. It is impossible to measure labour solely by the time which the labourer has spent in the factory or workshop or even at the lathe. Even our socialist state, with all its leanings towards standardisation, would have to reject such an evaluation of labour ; wages would have to be made dependant upon productivity. Thus the unit of value is not simply an amount of time worked, a labour day, for example ; it is a labour day of a given productivity, which productivity is assumed to be normal. This productivity is expressed as a certain quantity of the products produced by the worker : as a certain quantity of chopped-up logs, of sawn-up planks, of wooden posts, and so on. As, however, in a single undertaking which produces particular commodities, the labour of all sorts of specialists is employed, and as each of them does different kinds of work, it will be necessary to determine a suitable normal labour day for each type of work.

But within each individual concern there will also

be employed labour of varying quality, higher or lower. Along with labour which does not call for much training, and is always available in abundance, there will be labour which depends upon long years of training, and at times upon special gifts or at any rate upon natural aptitude. Such labour is only available in limited quantities and has to be used sparingly. Is it reasonable to evaluate it, as an item of daily expenditure, according to the same standards as have been set up for unskilled labour? This is impossible, however strongly our wages policy may lean towards standardisation. Even Marx points out that the time unit of unskilled work can only be considered as equal with that of skilled work if it is multiplied by a certain coefficient. But how is such a coefficient to be determined? We shall look in vain for the answer to this question in the works of Marx. It is often suggested that the problem can be solved by comparing the cost of training the skilled worker with that of the unskilled. To do this would hardly be a simple matter. If, however, the skill in question is the result of a natural gift—though not necessarily an exceptional one—the method proposed would be entirely inapplicable. It is clear therefore that the value of the coefficients will be hypothetical or even entirely arbitrary.

As, further, each concern obtains materials and machines from outside sources, it is clear that no production can be estimated unless there is at the same time an estimation of labour costs throughout the whole field of economic life and unless all types of labour and all qualities of labour are brought to a common denominator. Thus we see that the measurement of labour value, which appears to many people as something quite simple and objective, is in fact extremely complex and very far from objective. Although this method has been made obligatory in the Soviet state we must doubt whether in all its obscurity it is practicable.[1] And we cannot help asking how the consumer is to approach the matter. He does not know the conditions of production and does not want to know them ; how then is he to evaluate the economic goods he consumes in accordance with the Marxian principle laid down on the first page of Volume I of *Das Kapital*—i.e. in accordance with the labour expended on the goods ? Even for us, who have sought to make a more penetrating study of the production process, such an evaluation appears bewildering and arbitrary. But let us put aside such doubts, and let us assume that throughout the whole sphere of economic life and in all its innumerable undertakings, the evaluation of economic goods has somehow or other been carried out according to the amount of labour invested in them. Will such a calculation of labour value provide something equivalent in significance to the capitalist value calculations which are based upon data received from the free play of the market ?

The sum of the labour expenditure will correspond to a sort of debit of a capitalist account. But what will form the credit ? If we follow Marx, the result of production is measured by the labour value which the goods produced possess, not under the actual conditions of the production in question, but under conditions which must be regarded as normal ; and in fact the value of the products will be conditioned by the amount of socially-necessary time required for their production. But how shall we determine this socially-necessary time ?

[1] This decree was, in fact, never put into execution.

Marx gives no concrete guidance on this point. For our part we believe that any abstract construction of a normal production would be inadmissable. We shall, rather, have to regard as socially necessary the average costs of the separate undertakings.

Now let us suppose that we attempt to solve our problem in this manner—the manner which in our view conforms most closely with Marxian doctrine. In so far as a particular industry is represented by a single concern, it is evident that our labour calculation will not help at all. Nor will this method be any more effective in cases where the community is served by a small number of undertakings. But let us assume that a large number of undertakings are concerned in the production. Then what will be the outcome of our calculation ?

The undertakings will fall into two groups : in the one group the credit will outweigh the debit, and in the other the debit will outweigh the credit. Now in view of the large number of undertakings in question, it appears probable that we shall eventually receive valuable evidence as to which of these undertakings are rationally managed and which are not.

But such evidence could only claim to have any objective value in the rare cases, where all undertakings had approximately the same kind of structure ; that is to say, where the combination of various kinds and various qualities of labour was roughly the same in all undertakings. Only then would our calculation not suffer from the fact that we have reduced all types and all qualities of labour to a somewhat arbitrary labour unit. But in fact such similarities of structure are rare, and are in any case not very instructive. Of greater significance are the more numerous cases where radical differences of organisation appear as between the individual undertakings in a single branch of industry; that is to say, *where different combinations of types and qualities of labour are found among the different undertakings producing the same commodity. But it is precisely in these cases that the hypothetical character of the method by which we have reduced the various types and qualities of labour to a labour unit would prejudice the whole calculation.* If a concern gives wide employment to a type of labour which is scarce, and which is urgently required elsewhere for the execution of the community's most vital works, and if, in accordance with the socialist tendency towards standardisation, this type of work is paid for at rates little above those ruling for unskilled and abundantly available labour, so that the labour costs of the concern in question appear to be small, then it is nevertheless doubtful whether, in spite of these low costs, production should be carried on in the existing way. On the contrary, it might best be carried on in such a way that the types of labour most abundantly available to society were employed to the widest possible extent—whatever the statement of labour costs might show.

But the calculation of labour costs loses any sort of meaning when various undertakings operate under various natural conditions, and make use of capital in varying degrees. Let us consider a number of agricultural concerns which supply the market with the same products, but which are situated on lands of various fertility and further that, owing to the fact that they lie at various distances from the market, their transport costs are various. In such cases what significance has a comparison of labour costs in judging whether this or that concern is rationally organised? None at all; for no account is taken here of the differences in the quality of the land and in the distances from the market.

Let us further assume that some industrial product, say hemp rope, is made on the one hand in well-equipped rope factories and on the other hand by home-workers. In normal circumstances the statement of labour costs would show that the rope made in factories had cost less than that produced by the home industry. Does it follow from this that rope production should be promoted by enlarging the factories but not the home industry? This conclusion would be justified if the socialist society had unlimited capital at its disposal. Unfortunately neither the capitalist nor the socialist society are in such a position, even though many people seem to forget this fact. For this capital, available as it is in restricted quantities only, all sections of the economic community are in competition; whether it is more advantageous to invest it in rope factories or, for example, in the manufacture of agricultural machines, remains very questionable. Thus the fact that rope made in factories is, according to the labour account, less costly than that made by the home-workers is no reason to conclude that rope factories must be enlarged; if the community suffers from a shortage of capital then it is more likely that the rope factories will have to be liquidated after the existing machines are worn out and that the entire production of rope will have to be transferred to the home-workers. In actual fact our impoverished socialist state has again and again acted in this way, and it has been right to do so. Thus the fact that production always represents the co-operation of three factors—labour, capital and nature—retains its significance even under socialism and cannot be ignored. It is true that the creator of scientific socialism has attempted to ignore it in the first volume of *Das Kapital*, laying it down that labour alone is the basis of the exchange value of economic goods. But in the third volume he develops a further theory of exchange value which takes into account both the other factors of production ; this, however, is hardly compatible with the theory of value propounded in the first volume. And even if the later theory appears somewhat antiquated in the light of modern economics, it does not stand in such violent contrast to reality as the doctrine developed in the first volume.

IV

LABOUR COSTS AND THE MARKET PRICE

THE calculation of labour costs is thus quite unable to provide us with any useful guidance as to which of our undertakings were more or less rationally organised. We must also recognise that it cannot at best provide those decisive directives which are indispensable to the regulation of social production and which are provided, under capitalism, by value calculations. It is true that the capitalist is unable to see the books of his competitors, which remain a business secret so far as he is concerned. But he has no need whatever to see them, for the economic system itself provides him with direct information as to whether he can or cannot carry on his business under the given organisation. For against his prime costs stands the price of the goods he has produced, and this price is formed on the market, in one way or another, independently of the processes which have taken place in the factory. With us, on the other hand, the position is different. Against the prime costs of a commodity, there stands a figure which is derived from the prime costs themselves. The latter, however, are not the prime costs of the commodity as it is produced in the undertaking in question, but in all the undertakings supplying the market; for according to Marx's doctrine, these average costs represent the true value of the commodity. If a process which arises spontaneously be analysed, an error may easily pass unnoticed, but if we attempt consciously to reproduce this process, the defect becomes clearly evident.

Let us suppose that our socialist society has taken over from the capitalists all their lace factories and workshops. Let us further assume that the production of lace in a given factory calls for considerably less expenditure of labour than the "socially-necessary" labour time required for the same purpose. Now does it follow from this that the production of lace in the factory should be continued, and even increased, or not? In a society which cannot appease its hunger, has no clothes to wear, and no fuel to burn, such a question is superfluous. In such a society lace has lost its . . . "value". Here I must ask the reader's pardon. In analysing the theory of Marxian socialism I have so far considered it my duty to adhere to its terminology. But here I have had to make use of the expression "value" in a non-Marxian sense, for in the context in question it is simply impossible to find another word.

Take another example. We will suppose that a socialist society, which is blockaded from the rest of the world, has inherited from the capitalist society a large number of scythe factories. We will assume that some of these factories are not very productive, and manufacture scythes at a labour cost which is far in excess of the average standard. Should we close these factories? This question is again unnecessary, for it is clear that under the general economic conditions described we should be very willing to found further scythe factories, even if these were still less productive than those already in existence.

These two examples clearly demonstrate that there are value phenomena which Marxism either fails to recognise or consciously ignores. In fact, the value of which we have just been speaking is in no way directly dependent upon labour costs, but is rather a function of social needs. That this value can fluctuate independently of labour costs follows in the same way from the examples we have adduced. There has been no alteration in the organisation of the lace factories, and yet lace has lost its value ; there has been no alteration in the organisation of the scythe factories, and yet the value of scythes has risen. To this and only this phenomenon modern economics, which is founded upon the great achievements of Menger, Walras and Jevons, applies the idea of value ; while it regards that which Marx described as labour value solely as a component part of the costs. Both conceptions are sharply separated by the modern economists among Marxists—and indeed not without advantage to science. At the root of value phenomena lie subjective evaluations ; these are summed up and crystallised in the market price which reflects the intensity of the social need for commodities. Not only the rentier—as even Bucharin is prepared to admit—but also the proletarian satisfies his requirements with the sanction of the market prices. When he finds a warm overcoat on the market, side by side with the finest Brussels lace, not even the proletarian will be interested in how much labour was spent in the production of the coat as against that of the lace. On the contrary, he will only take into account the urgency of his needs. If the autumn weather has arrived he will pay the necessary price for the coat ; while for the lace he would only pay a very little, if he could fix

[1] The author argues here against the views put forward by Bucharin in his book, *Political Economy of the Leisure Class*. The name is applied by Bucharin to the so-called Austrian School of Economics.

the price of the lace. But the rentier with capital also visits the market. He has still less interest in the question of whether Brussels lace-makers have to work much or little ; on the other hand, he knows his wife's little weaknesses, and with his well-filled purse he is able to satisfy them ; thus he pays a price by which the Brussels lace-maker is more or less rewarded.

The manufacturer, in selling his goods, quotes the prices obtained on the market. In the capitalist society with its various propertied classes, these prices express the intensity of the demand for the goods. He enters them on the credit side of his account and only then is he able to judge the magnitude of his debit. In this way, by means of the market prices, capitalist society provides all productive organisations with powerful directives, and it compels them to regulate their expenditure in accordance with these prices. Therefore there arises, under the continuous pressure of these directives, a certain relation between the market prices and the production costs (though not between the market prices and the labour costs ; for labour is only one of the factors of production and consequently only one element of the production costs). It was only so long as science had not investigated the law of subjective evaluation, and of the objective expression of this evaluation in the market prices—it was only so long, that such penetrating thinkers as David Ricardo and Karl Marx, who in this respect was Ricardo's follower, could reach the erroneous conclusion that market prices are determined by the costs of production. Moreover, the father of this theory, David Ricardo, was unable to apply it logically in the wide field concerned with the price formation of agricultural products. On the contrary, he had to admit that prices represent in this case not the average, but the marginal costs of production. These marginal costs, however, are determined by the intensity of the demand. Here, therefore, he recognised the priority of demand in the formation of prices. Marx also recognised this theory of price formation in the case of agricultural products. Ricardo, in order not to undermine his own theory, represented this method of price formation as an exception, if an important one ; but modern economics recognises it as the only valid theory.

The formation of market prices is conditioned at any given moment by the requirements of society, and by these alone. Owing to the variability of consumption there can be no complete relationship between market prices and costs of production ; this could only be conceivable in a hypothetical " stationary economy ", with its " normal " prices. In the markets of our socialist republic goods are sold at prices which, as in other markets, do indeed correspond to the needs of the community ; but in no sense do they represent the costs of their production, for production is so disorganised that it is incapable of responding to the guidance which is offered by the market. Indeed, there are quantities of goods being sold on our market whose costs of production cannot be calculated, because the articles in question cannot be reproduced ; yet their prices are derived in an entirely rational manner from the given conditions of social demand.

But from what source is our socialist society to receive its directives for production, and in what manner are the managers of production to measure the intensity of social needs ? If we ourselves have recognised that the calculation of labour value might be able to show that production is relatively more profitable in this or that undertaking, *yet such calculation is nevertheless quite incapable of providing a measure by which we can decide whether an undertaking is economic at all.* Admittedly, in the example adduced above the state might declare categorically that the production of lace was not to be thought of. But this case is exceptional. It is the case of a state in unusually difficult circumstances and of an article which serves exclusively luxury purposes. In the great majority of cases the production of a commodity will pay with one set of costs and not with another. Now where shall the socialist state find a measure by which to decide whether the production is economic ?

The same question may be asked with equal force in respect to foreign trade. What is to be purchased abroad : flour, beans, herrings or possibly shoes and drugs ? Where is the mechanism by which our foreign trade commission is to obtain an understanding of the needs of the country ? How is it to know that one commodity price will be acceptable but that another will not ? These questions remain unanswered.

The Marxist Strumilin, who has sought to make a more penetrating study of the problem of economic calculation in the socialist state and who, unlike us, insists upon the objective significance of the calculation of labour value, has had nevertheless to agree that it is wholly inadequate for the purpose of regulating socialist production. He therefore considers it necessary to introduce the idea of the utility of economic goods : labour must be apportioned to the production of various economic goods in accordance with their utility. Thus we see that Strumilin is endeavouring to reconstruct in the socialist state the same mechanism which, in the opinion of modern economists, functions under capitalism. He has stated the problem rightly ; but his terminology remains Marxian. What he calls value is represented in modern economics by the idea of costs, and what he calls utility by the idea of value. But these distinctions are, of course, superficial.

In investigating the problem of the utility of economic goods, Strumilin discovers a phenomenon of which economic science has, of course, long been aware : that with the increase in the quantity of economic goods their utility is reduced. In this connection Strumilin recalls Fechner's psycho-physical law of the decreasing intensity of reaction with the repeated application of the stimulus. We were admittedly somewhat astonished, in reading Strumilin's exposition, that the esteemed economist had forgotten the doctrine of marginal utility, which represents, after all, an application of this psycho-physical law to the phenomena of economics. But perhaps even Strumilin belongs to that extensive circle of Russian intellectuals which has exalted Marx's *Kapital* into a sort of Holy Koran, and believes in accordance with the formula ascribed to Omar, that to repeat what is written in *Das Kapital* is superfluous, but to assert anything else is more superfluous still.

But however strange the expositions of Strumilin may appear—pretending as they do to reveal for the first time truths which have long been established by economic science—yet he has rightly apprehended the problem of regulating the socialist economic system.

Only he—unlike us—is convinced that it is quite possible to regulate economic life without taking account of the feeling of the market. On the contrary, he believes that the utility of economic goods may be computed *a priori* with the help of Daniel Bernoulli's well-known probability theorem regarding the so-called moral expectation. Here he overlooks the fact that this formula refers to money, that is, to the abstract equivalent of all economic goods. It would never have occurred to Bernoulli that his formula might be utilised in computing the decrease in value of concrete economic goods like bread, milk, wood, coats or galoshes, according to their quantity. The problem of investigating the laws which govern the consumption of all these goods has only recently been formulated and little has as yet been done towards its solution. At any rate we know that the intensity of the need for any economic good exhibits its own characteristic laws, that there are economic goods the demand for which is elastic and inelastic, and that the connection between the quantity of such goods and their utility cannot be expressed in any simple formula. Further, Strumilin has omitted to indicate how the utility of various economic goods may be reduced to a unit ; thus one will have to introduce coefficients which, as in the case of the comparison of skilled and unskilled labour, will be described as " certain " coefficients just because they are uncertain.

We are not surprised, therefore, that the Russian authorities, having followed Strumilin's suggestion and introduced the compulsory calculation of labour value, nevertheless did not wait for the result of these calculations. Indeed, not once did they make use of Bernoulli's formula in order to determine *a priori* the utility of the economic goods to be produced, but rather, in their desire to put the state enterprises into efficient operation, instructed the latter to be guided by the market.[1]

[1] Here the author alludes to the introduction of the N.E.P.

It is true that our market to-day is very imperfectly organised, and certainly much less so than in capitalistic times, yet it is better to be guided by this imperfect market than to work completely in the dark. Here, admittedly, our economic system forsakes the framework of socialism as Marxism conceives it.

But if it is impossible to operate socialism from the bottom upwards by means of suitable economic calculation, it is sought to direct it from the top downwards by means of a unitary economic plan based upon statistical data. Not only our governing economic control bodies, but also a considerable section of our intellectuals believe that such a solution of the problem is possible, and for this reason have criticised the government, which has not up till now been able to solve the problem. Thus Tschajanow is convinced that there will come a time when the economic Governing Board will be in a position to state how much milk, corn and pork the socialist state needs and how much may be spent on the production of each of these commodities ; so that the state, acting upon this information, will have tangible data to work upon in organising the state properties efficiently.

It is therefore necessary to examine the possibility of setting up a unitary economic plan for the state, and what its significance would be in regulating the socialist economy.

V

THE UNITARY PLAN OF THE SOCIALIST ECONOMY

THE unitary plan of the socialist economic system is the leading thought of Marxism. With the help of this plan socialism promises not only to take over the highly developed technique of capitalism intact, but hopes also, by further concentration of production and by selecting the most perfect forms of undertakings to raise it to the highest peak of efficiency; and it seeks to achieve a harmony between production and the needs of society which is beyond the reach of capitalism. As we have already said, Marxism refers repeatedly to the " Anarchy of Production ", and pledges itself to overcome this condition.

The capitalist society arose by way of a natural process of evolution; it had no theme, which it followed out according to a definite plan. Admittedly, the governments of capitalist countries have their economic policies, but these, if we exclude exceptional cases, consist entirely of part measures to influence economic life, and do not seek to thrust private interest and private enterprise out of their decisively important roles. To this extent it is possible to speak of " an anarchy of capitalist production ".

But this " anarchy "—i.e. the absence of any authoritative body which controls social relationships—does not necessarily signify that these relationships are in a chaotic condition. The truth is that capitalism also possesses certain regulating forces, and these function clearly and forcefully enough. Capitalist production, in fact, is controlled by the prices of the market.

Capitalism is a régime of free competition, and this competition finds expression both on the consumption goods market and on the production goods market. The free competition of consumers, who endeavour to satisfy their requirements as advantageously as possible, and the free competition of the producers, who seek to sell a definite quantity of goods on the market—these factors result in the price of the individual consumption goods finding a definite level, at which supply and demand are in equilibrium. This price represents the marginal utility which the economic goods in question have for society as a whole ; it is determined by the subjective evaluation and the purchasing power of all members of society.

The prices react sensitively to every change in supply and demand, just as the pointer of an accurate balance reacts with every alteration of the weights in the scales. The change in price may be brought about by demand. If, for example, the cold autumn weather comes unexpectedly early, buyers will experience a more urgent need for warm clothing ; but if this clothing is only available in quantities which are based upon the normal weather conditions, then the competition of consumers will force up prices. Another example : If a country which supplies the world market with a considerable amount of food has a bad harvest, the prices of the food will rise ; but as this food satisfies the necessities of life, then satisfaction of less urgent needs will be postponed and the prices of the consumption goods affected will fall. In the same way there may be a change in supply. We have just mentioned the dependence of the price of agricultural products upon fluctuations of the harvest. More often under capitalism, of course, there takes place an advance in methods of production, which makes it possible to produce a greater quantity of goods with the same expenditure. These goods can only be sold on the market at lower prices than have been realised hitherto. The market price of consumption goods then determines in its turn the funds which may be applied to the further production of each of these goods. But side by side with the consumption goods market there also exists a production goods market, on which there is competition among entrepreneurs. By free competition there is fixed for every means of production a price which corresponds to its marginal productivity, that is, to the extent to which the productivity of an enterprise is increased by the application of the means of production in question. In this way there arises a certain fluctuating equilibrium between social demand and the organisation of production. This equilibrium takes place now at one, now at another price level, now at this, now at that level of production. The point of equilibrium changes constantly as a result of pressure received now from the sphere of demand, now from the sphere of supply—of production. The process of price formation takes place spontaneously. Those who take part in it do not base their actions upon any theory, and seldom make use of statistical calculation; the entrepreneur does not regard either as indispensable to the solution of his immediate practical problems.

Yet it has to be admitted that the mechanism, taken as a whole, functions excellently. In spite of the fact that capitalism has neither theme nor plan, the needs of the community are satisfied with the greatest regularity; what is more, the market endeavours to meet the most refined requirements of the consumer and to respond to his most capricious moods.

Nevertheless, this quite automatic adjustment of production to consumption has its defects. These appear from time to time in the occurrence of over-production; that is to say, it becomes impossible to sell goods on the markets at a price which will cover production costs. Owing to the close connection of all economic elements in countries where industrial capitalism is developed, and the interdependence of these factors through the credit organisations, the crises which originate in some important branch of industry—most often in the sphere of production goods, i.e. so-called "heavy industries" —tend to develop into general industrial crises; indeed, spreading from one country to another, they become world crises. They ruin entrepreneurs, while among the workers there is mass unemployment with all its attendant misery.

Marx found the root cause of crises in faulty distribution, or, more accurately, in the fact that the condition of the worker was becoming worse; thus, he said, there arose a disproportion between society's growing power of production on the one hand and the purchasing power of the masses on the other. For this reason Marx expected that with the progress of capitalism crises would become even more severe, until the whole "Anarchy of Capitalism" would be led on to complete destruction.

This frightening prognosis has not in the meantime come to pass. Again and again capitalism overcomes the crises ; and then it experiences periods of prosperity, in which production is still greater than it was before. Moreover, in the country where capitalism is most widely developed—in England—crises have shown signs of becoming milder : that is to say, periods of industrial prosperity have exhibited a tendency to pass without violent shocks into periods of industrial depression. Thus industrial capitalism, in its higher stages, evolves with a pulsating rhythm. Here, naturally, we are not considering the post-war crises which are upon us now. It was obviously the industrial crises which led Marx to deny the market the power of regulating production.

The system proposed by scientific socialism for the regulation of production has nothing in common with what takes place under capitalism. The unitary plan of the socialist state is not the sum of the separate production plans as they are worked out by separate capitalist enterprises ; it has an altogether different basis. In the socialist state there is no market. All the functions of distribution are centralised in special boards, which act in accordance with the economic plan of the state. All the enterprises of a socialist state work for the " common stock-pot " ; out of which they too are provided.

Economic goods, and in particular the means of production, circulate in the socialist state without sale or purchase—without equivalent. It is not for nothing that all Russian students of the socialist economic system —like Bucharin, Tschajanow and Larin—have found in it features of the " natural " economy. In fact, we may ourselves make use of this comparison. We might put the socialist state side by side with the natural peasant community. In the latter also there are various kinds of useful land, different crops are cultivated, there are various branches of live-stock breeding, and all these economic elements stand in the closest connection to one another. Products of the fields and pasture lands are given to the animals ; the work of the horses, and the manure are made use of in the fields and in the kitchen gardens ; and this whole circulation of values from one economic department to another takes place without sale or purchase. Nor, in the peasant economy, is there any sharp line of demarcation between production and house-keeping—i.e. consumption—and this is also a characteristic of socialism.

This comparison, with which our students of socialism obviously console themselves, might indeed contribute something of significance to the problem of the regulation of the socialist economic system if—the two economic systems were comparable in size. The peasant organisation may be supervised and managed by a reasonably intelligent peasant. But is there any analogous intelligence capable of supervising intuitively the economic life of a small country, let alone that of Russia in all its immensity ? In such cases differences in degree become differences in kind.

The central organ of the socialist system—say the Supreme Economic Council—no longer possesses the sensitive barometer provided by the market prices. It will therefore be compelled, in order to bring production into harmony with social needs, first of all to gather together some sort of data which will enable it to determine what kind of goods and what quantity of them are required for the satisfaction of these needs ; then it will estimate the available means of production, among which the most significant will be that peculiar and unstable element, the labour power of the population. According to its estimate the Supreme Council will then apportion the available means of production among the most important branches of industry, and further, through the Governing Board, among the individual enterprises; the combination of the elements of production within the concerns will, however, have to be left to the local bodies.

"Socialism is the keeping of accounts": such is the slogan of to-day. And indeed, since the socialist state lacks the mechanism of the market prices, it must needs possess an enormous and unusually perfect statistical apparatus, an apparatus which embraces every aspect of social life, and which functions elastically and uninterruptedly, so that it may respond to every change in social life. But, of course, not even the most advanced western states possess so vast and expensive a statistical apparatus—let alone Russia. But we will not spend further time on these technical difficulties: let us pass on to the essential kernel of the problem.

Can the people's need for economic goods be determined *a priori*? We believe that this idea originated with Marx when he was impressed by the unhappy condition of the English workers in the first half of the past century; this condition is described in the celebrated work of his friend Engels. If capitalism—so runs his train of thought—can only provide subsistence for the workers, and even this, owing to the recurring periods of unemployment is not certain—then the working class has much to gain from socialism even if it can only guarantee him the means of existence.

More than half a century has passed since Ferdinand Lassalle announced so dramatically the "iron law of wages." For many reasons, however, among which the activities of the working class itself is not the least, the law of wages proved in fact to have been cast in a very much softer metal than iron. The workers of Western Europe, not to mention those of the New World, have long ceased to be content with the minimum quantity of economic goods which were absolutely necessary for the satisfaction of their elementary needs. Their needs cannot be measured ; the needs of civilised men as a whole cannot be measured *a priori*. Admittedly the satisfaction of their needs is restricted, thanks to the objective fact that the purchasing power of the workers is restricted.

In so far, therefore, as socialism aims not to depress but to raise the workers' standard of life its task cannot be to determine the minimum of economic goods required by the worker. Rather it will have to arrange economic goods in an enormous scale, in which every commodity will take its place in accordance with the consumers' evaluation of it. But then it would happen that one and the same economic good would appear at various places in the scale, for in certain quantities the good may well be absolutely indispensable, while further quantities of it lose their value. A skilled English workman, the member of a trade union, is accustomed to eat beefsteak with a glass of beer. Further, he likes to live outside the town in a little house and to come into town by the underground railway. Probably the English worker, like his American comrades, drives a Ford. Of course, the dockers, like other unskilled workers, have to live much more modestly ;—but the object of socialism is surely not to depress the workers' standard of living.

The worker naturally recognises the graduated value which the various economic goods have for him. Probably he is never willing to forgo the beefsteak or the first glass of beer; but the third and fourth glasses he would no doubt do without for the sake of a third room in his cottage if he has a family; but he might rather have a frock-coat or an evening dress for his wife than a further increase in the size of his dwelling. Besides, the workers, as civilised people, have various individual tastes, and they make demands accordingly on the capitalist market. On the market the infinitely various demand is summed up without any form of statistics.

But how shall we, as members of the socialist Supreme Economic Council, solve this problem *a priori*; what objective data do we possess for finding such a solution when there is no market upon which the consumers can give expression to the intensity of their demand? Even to forecast the most elementary requirements is, in the absence of a market, not so easy a matter as some people imagine it to be.

Let us begin with a consideration of foodstuffs. Let us assume that statistics provide us with accurate and up-to-date information as to the magnitude of the population and of its sex and age and occupational composition. Then physiology tells us how many calories are required by people of different ages and sexes in different kinds of work. Science tells us the minimum quantity of protein which the diet must contain; the remaining calories may be supplied by fats or carbohydrates. As we know the composition of foodstuffs necessary, it is possible to work out a ration which contains a sufficient number of calories, including protein. Nevertheless, it should be noticed that the value of these numerical calculations is very relative, for the number of calories an adult worker requires varies from 2,500 to 8,000 calories a day, according to the exertion called for by his work; moreover, the composition of the foods themselves fluctuates considerably—and it is naturally impossible to subject every portion to a chemical analysis. Yet the chief difficulty lies elsewhere.

In the nineties of last century the founder of the modern Energy Theory of Nourishment, the German physiologist Rubner, propounded the following principle: If, in the nourishment of a living creature, the minimum amount of energy necessary for the maintenance of its functions is supplied, then the organism is up to a point indifferent as to the form in which this energy is supplied. Since this proposition was put forward a quarter of a century has passed by. The Energy Theory of Nourishment has retained its significance, but with many modifications. We know that the organism requires a minimum of protein, but it appears that there is protein that is "full value" and protein which is not, and that it is the first kind which is indispensable. Further, it has been shown that the diet must necessarily contain lecithin, nuclein and vitamins, the latter so far not fully investigated. Again, it appears that the fats are of different nutritive value. Thus the population may be supplied with a sufficient quantity of calories and even of protein and yet suffer from widespread scurvy.

Now, it may well be replied, if the Supreme Economic Council, with all science at its disposal, is unable to put together a minimum ration, and to direct production accordingly—how is the simple citizen able to do it?

But the truth is that the latter needs no science. He responds to the state of his stomach and his body, and decides instinctively whether he wants meat or cheese or carrots or eggs. And his instinct does not deceive him. Now if there is a market, all these wants can be summed up, and the result of this process will provide directives for production which are more reliable than anything which statistics and physiology can offer.

But the estimation of the demand for food is by no means the most difficult task. How is it possible to work out the amount of wood the inhabitants of Petrograd require if they are not to die of cold ? The old standards are useless, as to-day we have only to heat single apartments or even single rooms in houses which are otherwise empty, but which were built for central heating. There are no new standards. But how, in any case, can the socialist society test the correctness of its *a priori* standards if there is no mechanism which indicates the intensity of the inhabitants' demand for wood ?

In the case of the standard for clothing the matter is even more difficult. For however we may insist, in view of the grave situation of the republic, that people only demand the satisfaction of their most elementary needs, it is impossible to distinguish here between the necessary and the conventional. We men may be satisfied with the most simple and monotonous clothes —but the women will instinctively refuse to be reconciled to such a state of affairs. Under a free exchange economy a woman will rather go without something to eat than something pretty to wear. Is our republic, even though its state is grave, to suppress this instinct ? We hardly think so. But in order to satisfy woman's demand for ribbons, lace and feathers, the republic will have to put off the production of other more necessary goods ; and to what extent shall these more necessary goods be sacrificed ?

The following objection may be made : does not even the capitalistic state undertake to satisfy the needs of certain groups of the population according to definite standards and does it not perform this task satisfactorily ? We have an excellent example of this in the provisioning of great armies. This, of course, is true enough, but the task there is vastly simplified. In an army we have to deal with a number of individuals of the same sex and age who are doing the same kind of work and are living a common life together. It is possible to observe this entire body of men as a whole and to gain an understanding of their point of view ; the consequences of supplying them with one or another form of food or clothing becomes clearly evident. Yet even the best-looked-after soldier would consider himself unlucky if he did not have a certain amount of money for himself ; for unless he did, it would mean that he was excluded from the exchange society and that he did not possess even a minimum of freedom to satisfy his own needs in his own way.

When communism here in Russia was at the height of its success it occurred to those in power that they might force upon the citizens a régime just as standardised and uniform as this. Hence the experiments with workers' homes, with compulsory billeting and with communal dining-rooms. But these attempts had very little success. The programme could not be carried out because it presupposed the abolishment of monogamy ; and although Madame Kollontaj was consistent enough to demand even this, the authorities could not bring themselves to take such a course. But even if the government had wanted to carry the experiment to its logical conclusion it would at best only have had the success of the " perfectly equipped barracks ".

Thus the socialist state is not in a position, even with the help of all its scientific theory and immense statistical apparatus, to measure the needs of its citizens or to reduce these needs to one level; for this reason it is unable to provide production with the guidance which it needs. But the weakest point of the socialist economic system lies in the efforts made by the socialist state to gather all the functions of distribution into the hands of its bureaucracy.

Under a free exchange economy every enterprise must fight unceasingly for its existence. It is in constant need of raw material, it has to replenish supplies of the means of production, the workers have to be paid and a return must be made on the invested capital. The means for satisfying all these demands are obtained from the community by the enterprise itself. It puts its wares on the market and if these wares are of value to the community and if the productivity of the concern is high then the market will return to the entrepreneur, in the form of the general value equivalent, sufficient funds for his purposes. With the proceeds the entrepreneur will himself obtain raw materials and new machines and pay his employees; the balance will form a profit, and if this is big enough he will devote a part of it to the extension of production. If the enterprise proves itself to be sound the community will give a credit to the entrepreneur and this will enable him to enlarge his business to an extent which would not have been possible with his own capital. On the other hand, if the productivity of the enterprise is low then the proceeds of his sales will not be sufficient to enable him to continue his business ; this is a *memento mori*, which means that the community will no longer permit its funds to be wasted in badly organised production. In short, the development of any capitalistic undertaking corresponds exactly to its productivity.

But under socialism the situation is fundamentally different ; here there exists no direct connection between the productivity of an undertaking and the supply of funds for its continuance. Under socialism two processes take place : first, the products of the enterprise flow into the " common stock-pot " and, secondly, the enterprise receives the means for further production out of the " common stock-pot ". Under socialism, the circulation of commodities is not effected by way of a series of sales and purchases, the course of which is independent of the wills of those who take part in them, but are merely determined by the conditions of the market. Members of the Supreme Economic Council may imagine that a connection exists between the flow of goods into the common stock-pot and the withdrawal of the means of production out of it. In reality, however, such a connection is very problematical.

Even if the state recommended the members of the Supreme Economic Council to maintain the connection between the two processes they would still be unable to do so, and for the reason already mentioned ; namely, that under socialism there is no general measure of value. Suppose that a Soviet estate has contributed so and so much milk, so and so many pounds of meat, so and so many bushels of grain. How many pounds of best quality seed, how much artificial manure or oil cake, how many head of breeding cattle or suits of clothes and how much fuel may the estate claim in return for its products? The attempt made by our esteemed expert on agricultural organisation, A. W. Tschajanow, has failed—this is not only our opinion but that of the Marxists. The attempt failed because, as we explained more fully above, in a society without markets the problem is insoluble.

If, therefore, members of the Supreme Economic Council were determined to maintain the principle that what an enterprise received must depend upon its productivity, and if, moreover, they were prepared to undertake the enormous work of investigating all the vast number of separate enterprises under their control, we should still not be in a position to provide an objective criterion by which they could assess these enterprises. Thus in the long run it must all depend upon the subjective evaluations of the officials. But this will make economic life subject to the influence of all sorts of political factors—an influence which in any case is much more in evidence in a socialist state, where political and economic power are identified, than in any other form of social organisation. For this reason it is possible that a socialist state, even if it finds itself in the greatest difficulties from an economic point of view, may nevertheless waste its funds on enterprises which have no economic justification at all, but which are supported by the government for political reasons.[1]

Even if the Supreme Economic Council recognises an enterprise as being economically sound, the further

[1] An allusion to the large-scale electrical undertakings during the famine years.

development of such an enterprise is not on that account assured. In a socialist state the work of distributing the various kinds of products and means of production must, as a form of divided labour, be entrusted to special authorities, that is to say to the Governing Boards (Glavki). These Governing Boards will be besieged with entrepreneurs competing among themselves for supplies, their weapons being petitions and exhortations, which cost nothing. All this is in strong contrast to the state of affairs which exists under capitalism, where competition takes place on a basis of prices. All the means of production which are thus requisitioned are, however, complementary, and it is therefore necessary that the decisions of the various Governing Boards with respect to each single undertaking shall tally. This process is infinitely more complicated than that which takes place under capitalism, where at worst the entrepreneur will have to increase his price to cover this or that means of production. It is no wonder, therefore, that in a socialist state the harmonious operation of an enterprise is not the rule but the exception. Too many cooks spoil the broth. It was universally recognised that the most productive naphtha deposits were those at Grosny, yet this did not prevent the area being left without the means of subsistence. And who can doubt that the Astrakhan fisheries are Russia's most important source of supply of fish ? Yet the fishers failed to obtain nets. Thus millions of pounds of fish have been lost simply because the homeworkers of Nizhni-Novgorod, who have always made the nets, were not supplied with the necessary materials. This may be ascribed to imperfect organisation, but could anything of the sort take place under the anarchy of capitalism ? Of course not. There can be no doubt that an entrepreneur in possession of any property so valuable as naphtha would always find the means of subsistence for those who produced the petroleum. In the same way the buyer of fishing-nets would always supply the home-workers with the necessary materials; if the worst came to the worst he would be prepared to pay another gold rouble for the pound of hemp, and this would naturally be refunded to him by the fishery owner of Astrakhan. This greater efficiency, of course, is not due to the fact that the entrepreneurs under capitalism are more intelligent and conscientious than are the servants of the Supreme Economic Council; it is due to the fact that the two forms of economic organisation are fundamentally different. The truth is that socialism lacks any mechanism for co-ordinating the separate processes of production. For this reason only those enterprises in the Soviet republic have retained their vitality which—in spite of very considerable opposition from the authorities—have retained their contact with the free market and have obtained supplies on their own account without relying upon the favour of the governing boards. What is more, those concerns which have not been fed by the state out of the common stock-pot have brought a greater return to the state than those which have existed entirely at its expense.

Now it may be asked whether capitalism itself does not display a tendency towards centralisation. It may be asked whether socialism is not following essentially the same path as that which has already been taken by capitalism. It is true that the Standard Oil Company controls all the petroleum in the United States and that the Steel Trust controls the entire metal industry; it is not without reason that our socialists, in trying to live up to their American ideal, are particularly fond of the word trust. But between the capitalist and socialist trust there is a fundamental difference of organisation. The capitalist trust is governed by the market, but the socialist trust ignores the market. The capitalist trust sells its products on the market and bargains for labour, engines, tools, metals and so on in free competition with other enterprises. It is distinguished from other capitalist enterprises only in the peculiar manner in which it determines the price of its goods. Yet even these prices are not determined simply at the caprice of the trust. For every increase of price results in a fall of demand and accordingly in an increase of expenditure on each unit of the product. The creation of a trust therefore does not necessarily signify high prices; on the contrary, trusts with their eye on the future often lower their prices below the level which at the moment is most profitable. This they do in order partly to accustom new sections of the people to the use of the product in question and also to prevent the sale of a competing product. Thus neither the aims of the trusts nor their economic organisation have anything in common with socialism.

With this we might really close our investigation. It is obvious that an economic system which possesses no mechanism for co-ordinating production with the needs of society cannot be maintained. Socialism overcomes the "anarchy of capitalist production" by substituting a condition of super anarchy; and in comparison with this "super anarchy" capitalism presents a picture of the utmost harmony. Here we might leave the matter if Marxism were nothing but a scientific theory.

Actually, however, Marxism as an economic programme has become the watchword of the greatest social movement of our time. This fact compels us to consider it in its other essential aspects.

VI

THE PROBLEM OF DISTRIBUTION UNDER SOCIALISM

THE socialist will no doubt assert that the problem of distribution can only become real under a system in which the propertied classes appropriate to themselves, in the form of interest and profit, the product of other people's labour. Such a problem, he will say, cannot exist under socialism.

But is it really possible, under socialism, for the worker to receive the value of the goods produced without any deduction being made for the capital which was used in the operation or for the natural resources which were employed (so far as these were not available in unlimited quantities). Would not this lead to a preposterous state of affairs and even to injustice ? Let us consider the problem in more detail.

Let us assume that a socialist society sends two groups of workers to the mines. Both groups work equally hard and with equal skill and both acquire an equal amount of ore. But from the ore produced in the one mine iron is obtained, while from the other platinum is obtained. Even under socialism platinum is valued higher than iron. Now will each group of workers be rewarded in proportion to the values they have produced or will they not ?

Or take another example. Suppose that a socialist

society puts at the disposal of two equal groups of agricultural labourers two pieces of land. Both groups work for a year with equal diligence and skill, but owing to differences in the quality of soil, the first piece of land yields one and a half times as much as the other. Even in a socialist society one and a half bushels of grain are worth more than one. Now will the community reward the two groups in accordance with the values they have created ?

In reply it may be argued that the platinum mine should be exploited more intensively than the iron mine and that the fertile piece of land should be worked more intensively than the less fertile ; in this way, it may be said, the marginal expenditure of labour will in both cases represent an equal productive value. But this will not alter the elementary fact that the group as a whole will gain more from the fertile piece of land than the group which works on the less fertile land. It is for this reason that the platinum mine yields a greater return under capitalism than the iron mine, and the fertile land yields a greater return than the less fertile land. Now let us return to an example which was mentioned above in another connection—to the case of the manufacture of rope in factories and by home-workers. A group of workers in the factory may produce more and perhaps better rope than an equal group of home-workers, even though the labour and skill of the two groups were the same. Even under socialism the rope will be valued according to its quantity and quality. Will the socialist society pay the two groups according to the value of the goods they have produced or will it not ?

There can be no doubt as to the answers to these questions, but socialists who wish to be thoroughly consistent will perhaps attempt to fence with them; they may argue that it is not in the least necessary that the workers' reward should depend upon the result of the production upon which he is engaged at the moment. But to carry this principle consistently into practice is impossible. Originally Russian communism leaned more towards the theory expressed in the words "each according to his abilities, to each according to his needs". But the state soon saw the harmful influence which this was having upon the intensity of work, and it had to introduce a wages system which aimed to maintain a certain proportion between service and reward. But if socialism, like capitalism, is compelled to differentiate in the payment of wages then clearly this differentiation can only be based upon the productivity of labour in so far as the productivity is determined by the intensity and the skill of the labour; but not in so far as the result of the labour depends upon certain natural conditions and a greater or less quantity of capital. But if this is the case, then even under socialism that part of the value of the product which is ascribed to labour must be distinguished from the parts which are ascribed to nature and to capital. Under capitalism these two parts are defined as interest or profit; if these words ring harshly in the ears of the socialists then some other description can be found for them, but this will not affect the kernel of the problem. Let us repeat the conclusion which was arrived at above when we were investigating the problem of the calculation of labour value: "the fact that production always represents the co-operation of three factors—labour, capital and nature retains its significance under socialism and cannot be ignored." *Thus interest and the return on capital are not historical but logical categories of the economic process.*

We are well aware that our views in this matter are fundamentally different not only from those of the communists and socialists but also from those of all the Russian intellectuals ; for the latter are all under the influence of scientific socialism. Even the late Tugan-Baranowskij, who first had the courage to develop the theory of marginal utility in the Marxian journal, *Sowremennyj Mir* (The Contemporary World), remained true to scientific socialism on the matter in question, and described interest and the return on capital as historical categories of the capitalist system. Thus we feel ourselves obliged to offer a still more detailed demonstration of our position. We shall endeavour to trace the tortuous zigzag course which might be taken by socialist thought in its attempt to break down the bonds imposed upon it by the conclusions we have reached.

In order to defend the basic idea of scientific socialism the following position would no doubt be taken up at once. It is not suggested that Marx ever maintained that the value of a definite commodity could be determined by the amount of labour put into it by the worker who happened to be engaged upon its production. Marx merely maintained that all values produced by the community were to be regarded as the labour product of the working class as a whole. Consequently every worker, assuming that he is normally diligent and of average skill, is to be regarded as the producer of an average value, a value which is dependent neither upon the influence of nature nor upon the fertilisation of the labour by capital. Now it would be quite possible to cite from the first volume of *Das Kapital*, in which goods always appear as "crystallised labour", a sufficient number of quotations to justify our own realistic interpretation of the Marxian theory—but in just the same way our opponents would be able to produce from Vol. III a sufficient number of extracts which favour their own more abstract interpretation. We believe, indeed, that the argument propounded in the first volume, while to-day out of date, is nevertheless distinguished by considerable force and cogency and has therefore exercised great influence upon the development of the science. On the other hand, the economic views set out in the third volume are less clear and on that account are of less scientific value. They are an expression of the doubt which Marx felt in the last period of his life as to the correctness of the realistic views propounded in the first volume, and of his attempt to modify them; he was not, however, in a position to remodel his ideas from the foundation upwards and for this reason presumably his whole work remained incomplete. In any case I am prepared to accept the point of view of my opponents and to assume that the abstract theory of value better represents the spirit of Marxism. Even this cannot undermine the conclusions we have reached.

Let us suppose that in two socialist republics the workers are equally diligent but that in the one there is a greater application of capital than in the other. The result of the labour is naturally different in the two republics. To what factor is this difference to be ascribed?

Or assume that in two socialist republics the workers are equally diligent and skilful and are equally well supplied with capital. One of them, however, possesses only brown coal, iron ore with a low metal content, barren sandy soil and no good natural harbours; while the second has the benefit of excellent anthracite, rich ore, fertile soil and good natural harbours. It is obvious that the result of labour will be different in the two republics. To what factor must this difference in the productivity of the two societies be ascribed?

Our theoretical reconstructions may take on a very concrete form, so that we are faced with very practical problems.

Let us assume that socialism is victorious throughout the world. Even so there will still be nations which are rich in capital and nations which are not. Let us imagine that the impoverished Russian workers ask their English comrades to lend them locomotives, machines, tools, and fertilisers, with the proposal that after twenty-five years all this capital or its equivalent shall be refunded. Interest on capital, of course, is regarded as a consequence of exploitation and it may be that the Russian workers, as enthusiastic Marxists, will be able to persuade the English (who are otherwise disinclined to accept abstract theory) that it does not become a proletariat to ask for interest—especially from another proletariat. But such a victory for the Russian point of view might have very unfavourable consequences for the Russians. The English workers might reply somewhat in this vein: "It is true that you need capital more urgently than we, but even we have not got too much of it. Our American comrades, after all, all have motor-cars, but our own motor-car factories lack as yet the necessary equipment. Besides, although we have made a beginning with our garden cities, they are far from completion, and in the meantime we have to live in dismal old cities which remind us of the bitter capitalist past. Are we now to postpone the satisfaction of all these needs for a generation? Don't forget that the capital we have does not belong to the *bourgeoisie* but represents our own sweat and blood." We must leave it to the Marxists to find an answer to these arguments: we ourselves are unable to do so. It is, in fact, evident that after the victory of the social revolution only two things will be possible: either the international circulation of capital will cease—and this would have a most injurious effect not only upon the development of the productive forces of mankind but also on the progress of culture; or interest on capital, so far as international transactions are concerned, will have to be regarded as just—whatever Marx may have said on the subject.

But now let us imagine another situation. A day will no doubt come when the English workers will make some such proposal as this to their Russian fellows: "Comrades, although you possess forests in Siberia, you are not in a position to exploit them properly because you lack the necessary capital, skilled labour and organisers. Let *us* exploit these forests." Indeed, the English workers might add, with a greater justice than had the Russians previously, and without even having to appeal to the words of the master: "You did not plant these forests, comrades, they grew from the soil of their own accord; perhaps it doesn't become *you* to demand a return for permitting us to exploit them." Yet it is more probable that such ideas will never enter the heads of the practical Englishmen who as yet will not have overcome the deep-rooted traditions of capitalism; it is more likely that they will offer to their Russian comrades some compensation in the form of interest and there is every probability that the Russians will not reject their offer.

The method of presentation which we have adopted in order to anticipate the objections of our opponents has proved to be especially fruitful, and for this reason : it has enabled us to eliminate from the cases we have investigated the question of the relations between the social classes, a question which, by affecting us emotionally, ordinarily obscures the whole setting of the problem. The logical character of interest and the return on capital as categories of any economic activity were displayed particularly clearly in the case of international transactions.

Now even if my imaginary antagonists were unable to discover in the store-house of scientific socialism any decisive objections to the conclusions we have just reached they might still make the following assertion with regard to profit : namely, that if profit is indeed a logical category of the economic process it must still in the long run be awarded to labour, for capital, in the last resort, is a product of labour. Yet even this assertion of scientific socialism must be rejected.

Once more let us exclude from our discussion, in order to avoid obscuring the problem, the question of social relations. Let us assume that in two socialist republics there exist similar natural conditions, equal supplies of capital, and workers whose diligence and ability are the same. Let us assume that there is only one difference between the two states. In the one the workers have inherited from the age of capitalism a virtue which is very common under capitalism—prudence. Thanks to this characteristic they succeed not only in preserving the old capital but also in increasing it from year to year.

On the other hand, the workers in the second republic suffer from a certain lack of prudence, and for this reason, their capital grows less and less. If this course of things continues, the workers in the first republic will grow perpetually richer and it will be more and more easy for them to increase their capital. On the other hand, the workers of the second republic, although they are just as diligent and skilful, will grow ever poorer; and if eventually need teaches them wisdom it will be difficult, in the face of the low productivity of their impoverished economy, to improve their condition. Of course, the wealthy but peaceful socialist republic will not now, as not infrequently happened under capitalism, make war upon its neighbour with a view to subjecting it in the imperialistic manner. It is more likely that after it had saturated its own system with capital it would offer the surplus to the impoverished country at a certain rate of interest. In this way capital lent at interest would help an impoverished nation out of the difficulties which it had brought upon itself by its own folly.

This example, which, as before, we have intentionally chosen in order that the question of social relations may not confuse the issue, proves clearly that although labour is an indispensable factor in every production and consequently in the production of capital, production and consequently labour also do not, as such, create capital. In order to create or even to preserve capital something else is necessary—perhaps we may call it "abstinence". But Lassalle has already made mock of this expression with the help of an illustration depicting a pile of capitalist ascetics, with Rothschild on the top, who by their "abstinence" create the chief mass of capital.

Those who manage to save capital out of a modest income must indeed practise self-control; but the greater the income, the less appropriate is the word self-control, for in this case the amassing of capital demands only prudence and calculation. The English economists have introduced a still more objective description—"waiting". But in any case we are not concerned with modes of expression; our aim is to show that capital is a special category of economic life which cannot be traced back simply to labour or to production.

Thus we see that the adherents of economic socialism have gone too far in their opposition to the individual appropriation of interest and profit, for they entirely deny to interest and profit the character of logical economic categories and also reject the idea of an origin of capital which is not identical with labour and production. The truth is that no rational economic organisation is possible without the division of the value produced among the three categories of income: wages, profit and rent.

We have made a long theoretical digression. Nevertheless, facts have emerged from it which are of value to practical socialism though not, of course, to Marxist doctrine. Our experience since the revolution is already showing that the attempt of communism to make the reward of labour independent of its results must necessarily paralyse the energy of the workers—to-day, therefore, our republic is endeavouring to make wages as strictly as possible proportional to services rendered. At the same time it becomes quite impossible to maintain the point of view that the worker is entitled to claim the full product of his labour. The question has become a very real one since our republic, breaking away from the Marxian conception of socialism, has permitted separate factories to sell their products on the market. Now are the workers in a nationalised tobacco factory entitled to claim the full proceeds of the production with the deduction only of a part for the purpose of paying off the capital ? From the Marxian point of view the answer would be in the affirmative, but from the point of view developed here it would have to be in the negative. As, in fact, the capital belongs to the republic, representing the sum of the workers and as the productivity of labour depends upon capital, then the republic is entitled to demand compensation from the workers for the facilities offered, for the opportunity granted to them of applying their labour in the factory ; the republic, in fact, is entitled to demand interest on capital. If the republic provides the workers with land to be worked and held in usufruct, then it is justified in insisting upon the payment of a rent.

The fact that the Marxian doctrine cannot be maintained under the New Economic Policy becomes plainer still if we consider the leasing of nationalised factories to private enterprise. If the workers are entitled to demand for themselves the full product of labour, then their rights are certainly infringed if an entrepreneur is thrust upon them and exploits them. And further, by what right does the Republic demand the payment of rent from this entrepreneur, a payment which naturally still further diminishes the earnings of the workers ? To tell the latter that our Republic was a workers' state would be poor consolation, for the funds of the working-class as a whole are after all not the same thing as the funds of the workers in question.

From our point of view, however, the Republic is guilty of no infringement of the rights of the workers in demanding the payment of rent from the entrepreneur. But in order to determine more exactly the amount of the rent we must analyse capitalist profit. According to modern economics, this profit is not a supply of " surplus value ", but consists of three fairly clearly defined elements : compensation for the use of capital, compensation for subjective and objective risk, and profits of management. Now it is clear that the state is entitled to demand compensation for the use of the capital, for the subjective risk, and for part of the objective risk ; but the profits of management and part also of the compensation for the objective risk are left with the entrepreneur. In all this, naturally, there is not a trace of Marxism, though elements of socialism in the wider sense are there ; for the unearned forms of income which, however, do not include the profits of management, are retained by society.

Besides, it must be admitted that the Republic may very well need both the rent and the interest on capital. The socialist state does after all carry the chief risk of production and its slightest error may destroy its original capital. Still more important is the fact that the whole structure of socialist society is such that, among its members, the impulse to save is blunted. Thus the formation of capital, which under an individualistic régime is so powerful a process, is strangled at the roots. For this reason the socialist community must take upon itself the task of further reproducing capital ; a task which may indeed be beyond its powers. Then again such a community will have to satisfy the collective needs of its members, and in particular their cultural needs, to a considerably greater extent than was the case under capitalism ; for under capitalism these cultural needs were satisfied to a large extent out of private resources and by private initiative. Now it is clear that the funds required for all these purposes cannot be derived from taxes alone. Besides, taxes are easier to collect in a capitalist society where a considerable portion of the national income goes to a limited group of people than in a society in which the tendency towards standardisation has led to a division of the national income into small equal parts.

Even Marx has referred in his letters to the necessity of making deductions from wages with a view to providing for the further reproduction of capital and for the cultural requirements of the people. Only he has made no statement as to the exact extent to which these deductions can justly be made.

Our conclusions with regard to interest and profit are also of significance in a consideration of co-operation, which is related to socialism. Co-operation is founded above all on the theories of scientific socialism, and for this reason its position *vis-à-vis* the labour question is very ambiguous.

VII

ECONOMIC FREEDOM AND SOCIALISM

ENGELS asserts that " Socialism is a leap from the realm of necessity into the realm of freedom ".

In order to reach the Catholic paradise it is necessary to pass through purgatory ; in order to reach the socialist realm of freedom it is necessary to pass through the dictatorship of the proletariat. Thus in the first place the social revolution brings us only to dictatorship.

The attitude of the dictatorship of the proletariat to the principle of personal liberty arises out of the idea of dictatorship itself and has been made sufficiently clear by the experiences of Russia. It is quite vain to attempt, as did Kautsky and the Russian Menschewiki, to obscure this simple and concrete matter by approximating the Marxian dictatorship to democracy. Marx himself knew very well how to keep these two ideas separate : when he chose the word " dictatorship " in order to characterise the transition period between capitalism and socialism, he did not do so merely *pour épater le bourgois,* for he regarded the matter as much too serious for that.

At the same time, the dictatorship régime, according to the Marxian view, should be only transitory. Bucharin, it is true, endeavours to persuade us, in his *Economics of the Transition Period,* that the reconstruction of society will require not years but decades ; and indeed the

Russian experience seems to show that such a reconstruction cannot be undertaken precipitately.

But sooner or later, when the dictatorship of the proletariat has finally overcome the class formation of society, this dictatorship will, according to the Marxian conception, disappear of its own accord ; what is more, the death of the state will then set in. Scientific socialism asserts that the state is nothing but the organisation of class domination. Under democracy the *bourgeoisie* dominates the proletariat through the instrument of the state ; now, under the dictatorship of the proletariat, the reverse process will take place. After the class formation of society has entirely disappeared, however, the state will become superfluous. Under socialism there will be no domination of men by men ; there will only be the organisation of production—the domination of things by men, of nature by men. Socialism leads humanity, though by quite another path, towards the same happy stateless condition that is promised by anarchism. On closer inspection, however, this entire notion of a stateless condition gives rise to grave doubts. Is it really true that the socialist society only knows a domination of men over nature ? Let us assume that I am the owner of a house in a bourgeois society. It is surely clear that my ownership is not essentially a relation between myself and a physical entity—a house. Essentially it is a relation between me and my fellow citizens with regard to the house. When I say that the house belongs to me I mean that my fellow citizens cannot use the house without my permission. But analogous relationships will retain exactly the same legal character under socialism. Here, however, the place of the individual house-owner is taken by society ; society through its legal organs has the right to dispose of the house while the other citizens have no such right.

Just as little is the organisation of production concerned with the relation of men to nature. It may be possible to assert something of the sort with regard to isolated peasant farms ; but such an assertion has no important bearing upon the socialist economy ; for the latter is based upon the large-scale concern, and presupposes the strongest differentiation and the most all-embracing integration of the work of the citizens, and also the utmost co-ordination of all branches of economic life. At any rate it is clear that a socialist society does not require less discipline from its members than does a capitalist society. On the contrary, there will exist under socialism very complicated relations between individual citizens as the result of the now inevitable hierarchy in production. Moreover, there is no reason to assume that every citizen will identify his private interests with the interests of society as a whole. Supposing, however, that complicated legal relationships exist in a society and that there is conflict, if not between social classes at least between individuals and between individuals and the community, then a coercive organisation must be present, in order to uphold the legal order in question : and this coercive organisation will be the state. This conclusion can hardly be disputed unless mankind, after the victory of socialism, is transformed collectively and individually into angels. Thus the idea of a stateless condition, even in a socialist society, proves to be illusory. It is true that state coercion may become more moderate ; but even the democratic state of to-day strives for such moderation—and not without success.

We have no wish to blame socialism for the fact that Marx's promise as to a stateless existence cannot be realised. But we cannot accept without hesitation the promises made by scientific socialism with regard to a realm of liberty on earth ; rather we must ask ourselves whether socialism offers sufficient economic grounds for supposing that this condition can be achieved.

Let us first consider the extent to which socialism is compatible with the principle of economic freedom, that is to say with the three fundamental institutions : freedom of economic initiative, freedom in the organisation of consumption and freedom of labour.

While the freedom of economic initiative is of great value to the individual, it may be of even greater importance to society as a whole. The extraordinary development of the productive forces under capitalism is very closely connected with the principle of economic freedom and the principle of free competition. In a free exchange economy, no productive organisation has the monopoly of providing society with any particular service. On the contrary, any organisation may be supplanted by any other which provides the services in question better and cheaper. Upon this fact is founded economic progress.

Now it is easy to see that conditions under socialism are much less favourable to free initiative. In the first place, where wages are more or less equal, many of the motives which under capitalism stimulate enterprise must disappear. Scientific discoveries, it is true, are not made out of a desire for profit but in answer to humanity's unquenchable thirst for truth. In the case of inventions the scientific interest recedes in favour of practical motives. But neither scientists nor even inventors are directly responsible for economic progress ; it is the organisers and practical men who stimulate development. Their task lies neither in the sphere of scientific discovery nor of invention. Nor, as a rule, are they concerned with the practical exploitation of inventions ; their problem is to discover the most successful combination of the factors of production with a view to producing this or that commodity at the least cost ; to find cheaper and more perfect means of satisfying society's needs ; or, finally, to discover new social needs and cheap methods of satisfying them. The entrepreneur, therefore, being mainly concerned with the material wants of men can naturally not be guided by idealistic motives—his activity is stimulated by the desire for personal enrichment.

Under socialism, this motive is suppressed, for it runs contrary to the socialist idea of equality. But even if the spirit of enterprise did not completely disappear under socialism it would only find expression with great difficulty owing to the completely bureaucratic form taken by economic life. It may be objected that the socialist society would put its undertakings in the charge of the most capable organisers and that these organisers would devote the most careful attention to all proposals for technical improvements. But even socialism offers no guarantee against nepotism ; while the impossibility of exact calculations of value will make it extremely difficult for the higher officials to assess the worth of the proposed innovations. Even supposing, however, that the highest posts were filled in the best possible manner, there would still remain the danger that each innovation could only be tested in a definite place. How much more effective is capitalism in this connection. Competition among individual capitalists impels them to take up every successful innovation which is offered, and to do so as quickly as possible. Indeed, the inventor may have capital himself or he may be in a position to obtain credit in order to carry out his idea.

If therefore the socialist organisation succeeded in assuming stable forms it would be distinguished by immense indolence and conservatism. It would offer nothing which could be compared to the unceasing movement of economic life under capitalism.

If socialism cannot provide scope for initiative in the sphere of production, still less is it in a position to ensure freedom in the sphere of consumption. Socialism organises production without being guided by the desires of the consumers as manifested on the market; this fact alone encourages a tendency towards a trustee-authoritarian distribution of consumption goods. Admittedly a considerable number of Marxists are accustomed to contrast themselves, as socialists in the real sense of the word, with the communists who believe in an authoritarian distribution of consumption goods. But the truth is that in this connection a deep inner union may be perceived between socialism and communism. It was not for nothing that Marx and Engels described their famous manifesto as "the communist manifesto". And it was not for nothing that the active sections of the Russian social democrats rechristened themselves at the time of the social revolution as a communist party.

The Marxists who reject communism imagine that the socialist state would pay for the labour of its citizens by means of certificates and that the owners of these certificates would be able to exchange them at their free discretion for the economic goods they require. But as prices in a socialist society are fixed independently of the market there can exist no equilibrium between supply and demand. On the contrary, the price of many economic goods will be too low and the demand for them will therefore exceed the supply, while the price of other goods will be much too high so that the supply will exceed the demand. Now clearly it would be absurd to supply the scarce goods to just those people who happened to discover them first but to allow the goods of which there is a surplus to rot in the shops. Thus it only remains for the state to distribute both kinds of goods.

It may be objected that such a disproportion between supply and demand will be only transitory and that production, in the course of economic development, will adjust itself to the demand. But even under capitalism, where such an adjustment is to the vital interest of the entrepreneurs, the equilibrium between supply and demand can only be achieved by a perpetual and at times very considerable fluctuation of prices. How then may we hope that the much clumsier socialist economic machine, working with fixed prices, will be able to achieve such an equilibrium? Thus the authoritarian distribution of consumption goods must constitute an essential feature of the socialist system, definitely rejecting, as it does, the regulation of prices by means of market trading. In Soviet Russia there is still another reason for a scrupulous distribution of consumption goods: the extreme exhaustion of a country in which the means of existence are only available in very limited quantities. But even if the country succeeded in improving its condition it would still—assuming the continuance of socialism—have to retain this method of distribution;

the only effect of such an improvement would be that rations would be less inadequate.

The authoritarian distribution of consumption goods puts an end to the free satisfaction of needs. Such a distribution means that I must eat the food—and it may be excellent enough—which is set before me by the communal food centre ; that I am not entitled to choose the sort of furniture I like ; that a woman is not permitted to wear the hat which suits her best.

This method of distributing consumption goods, moreover, will make it impossible to satisfy our higher spiritual needs, in which, after all, there is a material substratum. It must be emphasised here that socialism which seeks to draw a distinction between itself and communism could, in the event of its realisation, at best only guarantee the satisfaction of the elementary needs ; it could in no way secure the satisfaction of our higher requirements. If the entire printing industry is taken over by the state, then it is difficult to imagine that the latter would publish works say on metaphysical philosophy even if the citizens were intensely interested in them ; for the state would consider such works as being at best useless. In the same way a state with anti-religious leanings would not be likely to build churches, and so on.[1]

[1] " Eat what you can get ! " This laconic aphorism from Tchekov's story, " The Charge-book ", was used by Strumilin to describe the existing system of distribution in Russia, when writing in *Ekonomitscheskaja Zhiznj* at the end of the year 1920. I myself had chosen the same aphorism in lecturing on the communist distributing system three months earlier. This astounding similarity of judgment and choice of expression between two such differently minded writers suggests that the phrase deserved to be placed at the head of Lenin's articles in which he argues so eloquently for the payment of labour in kind and the abolition of a money economy, on both of which principles this distribution system is based. (This note was suppressed by the censor.)

The authoritarian distribution of economic goods—as is equally the case with the bureaucratising of economic life generally—not only imposes the strictest limits upon the citizens' freedom but also depresses the productivity of society to a low level. If a definite quantity of economic goods are authoritatively distributed among a definite number of people, then their needs will not be so well satisfied as would be the case if these same people were enabled to divide the goods freely among themselves according to their different requirements. When all is said and done, things do not of their own accord become economic goods of a certain value, nor even do they do so on account of the labour cost inherent in them (as the Marxists think); they do so simply and solely in so far as they satisfy the present needs of mankind. But when a distributive organisation fails to take account of the needs of the individuals of which society consists, that is equivalent to a reduction of productivity.

In addition, the experience of Russia has shown clearly enough that the authoritative distribution of goods is the most clumsy and expensive method which can be conceived.

At the time of the social revolution the Russian Bolshevists rightly grasped the connection between communism and socialism in the sense mentioned above; but to the last, they were not clear as to the essential connection between socialism and the coercive organisation of labour. The need for such an organisation arose quite unexpectedly, so far as the party in power were concerned, in the midst of their socialist construction, and they were inclined to regard this development as a transitory measure connected with the events of war. Only one of the most determined and consistent Russian communist leaders recognised intuitively the essential connection which exists here and affirmed it.[1] Yet it is not difficult to see that the connection between socialism and communism and the coercive organisation of labour is not fortuitous but fundamental.

Under a free exchange economy the price of an article rises where there is a scarcity and sinks where there is a surplus. The price movement influences the wages paid in the different branches of industry and this, in its turn, brings about a new distribution of labour among the various branches of production—a distribution which is in accordance with the actual needs of society. Under socialism, on the other hand, the fluctuations of demand for goods do not affect their prices while the payment of wages is governed by the principle of equality. Thus the socialist economy possesses no mechanism capable of effecting a spontaneous distribution of labour among the different branches of production according to the needs of society. But as such a distribution is, of course, a social necessity it only remains to adopt coercive measures. For this reason the labour army appeared under socialism as an ideal form of labour organisation.

Is it necessary to-day, in the twentieth century, to prove that forced labour is less productive than free ?

The problem of political freedom takes us beyond the scope of our study. Yet from what has been said already the attitude of socialism to this aspect of freedom should at once be clear. Scientific socialism maintains—and in our opinion quite justly—that institutions having a standing under public law cannot exist in a vacuum but must possess an economic basis. Capitalist society has proclaimed the rights of men and citizens, and this

[1] The author alludes to Leo Trotsky.

declaration is closely related to the economic foundations of capitalism : to free competition, to the free organisation of consumption, to free labour and, above all, to the principle of private property. As long as these foundations stand firm, the declaration of rights will remain in force. Under socialism, on the other hand, the economic presuppositions of individual freedom in general and of political freedom in particular are lacking ; our communists therefore quite logically reject these liberties as an institution of bourgeois society.

It is true that socialism, in order to make up for this loss of freedom, asserts that the formal freedom of a bourgeois society actually conceals a negation of freedom ; that it conceals the oppression of the economically weak by the economically strong. If this socialist criticism of capitalist freedom is not altogether justified, there is nevertheless much truth in it. For this reason, modern democracies have also renounced the bourgeois principle, *laissez faire, laissez passer* ; many modifications have already been introduced into the system of free exchange, and the object of these modifications is to strengthen the position of the economically weak ; many other improvements remain to be made. But of course the cause of personal freedom will not gain by the fact that it is now to be entirely abolished, both formally and in essence.[1]

[1] The impossibility of combining the socialist order of society with individual liberty was clear to all who troubled to inquire more closely into its structure, even when they started from the premisses of scientific socialism. This impossibility was attested both by such avowed opponents of socialism as Spencer and Eugen Richter and so warm an admirer as Tugan-Baranowskij who dedicated his swan-song to the cause. " Centralisation, which dominates the socialist state," he wrote, " presupposes the strict obedience of the individual to the com-

Then what do Marx and Engels mean when they describe socialism as a " realm of freedom " ? These are no mere words which have slipped out by accident ; the idea is one of the foundations of their doctrine of the society of the future.

Their meaning is as follows : The development of capitalist society is an elemental process. Every member of such a society has, it is true, a share in determining the conditions of the capitalist economy ; nevertheless, the capitalist economy is—both to society and to the individual—something " objectively given ", which is dependent neither on the will of society nor of the individual. In times of prosperity every manufacturer is paving the way for the industrial crisis which must inevitably follow such prosperity, and although he himself will feel the effect of the crisis, he can in no way alter his mode of conduct. No more can capitalist society as a whole prevent the industrial crisis. To this extent the capitalist economy is a realm of necessity.

Under socialism, on the other hand, society takes its destiny into its own hands ; it organises the economic system according to a national unitary plan. Under socialism economic life is subject not to blind forces but to the will of society. Here there can be no unexpected events, for even economic development is governed by the common will. To this extent socialism is a " realm of freedom ".

mands of the central power and the transference to it of all economic initiative and all responsibility for the regular functioning of the economic system. Hence it does not correspond to the ideal of the greatest possible liberty of the individual personality " (*Socialism as a Positive Doctrine*, Russian edition, p. 83). And being as he was a devotee of socialism, Tugan-Baranowskij naturally expresses himself with comparative mildness.

Unfortunately Marx and Engels did not engage in a more thorough examination of the social order which they sought to bring about by revolutionary means ; for this reason the idea of the " realm of freedom " was not determined, so far as they are concerned, in greater detail.

But it is clear that a socialist society is not a realm of freedom for the individual. Quite the contrary : the individual renounces all liberty in order that society may be able to dispose over its own destiny. But through what instrument is society able to accomplish this determination of its own destiny ? Clearly through the state. We must therefore reject decisively Marx's notion that under socialism the state would not exist. It is precisely under socialism that the state appears in all its omnipotence, not only in the political but also in the economic spheres of life. The Leviathan of Hobbes, which absorbs the individuality utterly, is represented not by the former monarchist state of the west nor by the democratic state of to-day—it is represented by the socialist state.

VIII

THE SUBJECTIVE FACTORS OF THE SOCIALIST ECONOMIC SYSTEM

MANY socialists maintain that in any general evaluation of the socialist economy account must be taken of the extraordinary increase in the productivity of labour which is to be expected. Such an increase, they assert, must follow from the fact that the antagonism between workers and entrepreneurs will have disappeared. Even Marx expected a change in the psychology of the worker under the influence of the new economic order, even though the effect of this influence would not be immediate. He expected that the members of a socialist society would become with time " socially minded ", that they would renounce the relation between reward and labour and accept the true communist principle which is expressed in the words, " everyone according to his abilities, everyone according to his needs ". Indeed, Marx connected this new social psychology with the idea of the stateless existence of the future society.

Actually, however, there is no reason to assume that the social revolution, as such, should have a favourable effect upon the intensity of labour. The intensified class war which precedes the revolution may well have a favourable psychological effect on the workers, for it strengthens their sense of class solidarity and their capacity for self-sacrifice. But it cannot increase the attention and energy which the worker devotes to his productive activities. Even if the social revolution does dispose of the conflict between entrepreneur and worker in the sphere of production, yet the transference of production into the hands of society does not mean that the worker consciously identifies his own interests with those of society. " The worker in a state factory," says M. Tugan-Baranowskij,[1] " has no motive for working with more than average intensity or for producing more than average results." The social revolution in setting aside the existing hierarchy must at the same time destroy the existing discipline of labour, and great efforts will have to be made by the socialist state in order to restore this discipline. But in order to achieve this it will have to return to approximately the same hierarchical organisation of large-scale industry as existed before. To attempt immediately after the revolution to impose upon the working class the communist principle, " everyone according to his abilities, everyone according to his needs ", is bound to have the most deleterious effect upon the productivity of labour ; our own republic's experience in this connection was bitter, and to-day it is striving with all its power to introduce the strictest possible proportionality between wages and the productivity of labour.

But it is not only immediately after the social revolution that no fundamental changes are to be expected in the psychology of the workers ; in any work of economic construction one must take as a general principle that man is guided in his economic life by motives of egotism. Our republic suffered much from the fact that it ignored this principle. In asserting that this fundamental principle of classical economics holds good under socialism

[1] *Socialism as a Positive Doctrine*, *op. cit.*, p. 88.

we do not mean to deny the significance of altruistic motives in social life. But human beings display a capacity for disinterested action and self-sacrifice only in certain circumstances and cases : when engaged in creative work of the highest order, when fighting for values held to be imperishable (even though others may regard these values as fictions) and finally in intimate life. It would be a mistake to expect men to bake bread, sole shoes or sew shirts day after day for disinterested motives, and to expect them to do this not for their nearest and dearest but for unknown members of society whom they may never even see. It is true that the Russian proletariat displayed extraordinary heroism in its fight for its social ideal ; but at the bench it works with an intensity which corresponds to the wages it receives. And this is true even of the spiritual giants among men. Spinosa wrote his essays under the pressure of a deep inner urge and he would still have done so if he had been threatened with prison on account of his work ; nevertheless, he was prepared to polish glasses for payment. And I shall not wound the religious susceptibilities of my readers if I say this : that the creator of the religion of love accepted the martyrdom of the cross for the sake of his teaching, but that if at any time he worked as a carpenter, he would have worked for payment—at least if the spirit of man was within him. If in any work of economic construction we do not proceed upon the basis of this fundamental economic principle, then we have utterly mistaken human nature. The progress of culture is expressed in this fact, among others—that the worker fulfils his obligations as conscientiously as possible. But such progress can be achieved under capitalism just as much as under socialism.

It was hoped that under socialism there would be an enormous increase in the productivity of the community ; but this hope proved to be false and the very opposite took place. Many socialists, right wing as well as left, light-heartedly assigned the responsibility for this failure to the working class. Now it was said that the workers had shown themselves unprepared, now that they were still subject to the overwhelming influence of the alleged petty bourgeois environment—the latter having become for socialist writers the universal scapegoat. We for our part consider that it is hardly just to discover in the psychology of the working class the cause of our failure. It is true that no miracles occurred after the social revolution, but then, there was no reason to expect them. If the efficiency of the workers fell away disastrously, this deterioration corresponded entirely to the unfavourable external conditions ; to the complete disorganisation of the economic system and in particular to the low standard of life. On the other hand, there is in principle no reason to doubt that the worker will be less diligent at the bench of a socialist factory than in a capitalist factory.

If, however, the construction of a socialist system is threatened by subjective factors, the danger lies not in the psychology of the working class but in the psychology of the organisers of production.

A characteristic feature of scientific socialism is its one-sided view of production, which it regards merely as a process of mechanical work. Marxism denies that the merchant plays an extremely important part under capitalism ; it sees in the merchant only a parasite. It also denies the importance of the economic managers of production, and regards these merely as specialists in the appropriation of surplus value. Finally, Marx underestimates the part played by the technical organisers of production.

Accordingly the fate of the economic and even of the technical managers after the Russian revolution was wretched in the extreme. The latter were originally to be replaced by boards of politically enlightened workers and the former by intellectuals who were more or less well acquainted with Marx's *Das Kapital.* Only after bitter disappointment did the state realise that the matter was by no means so easy as it had imagined. The economic and technical managers of production were rehabilitated and put back into their places as "spezy" (specialists).

We cannot, however, expect, either from the old or from the new specialists, the same service that they were able to give under capitalism. The truth is that successful production depends above all upon organisation, not only in the technical but also in the economic sense; the care and preservation of original capital, the careful use of raw material, a successful combination of labour and capital. The discovery of suitable sources of supply and good markets—these factors play the decisive part in successful production, and without them even the most diligent and skilful performance on the part of the workers will avail nothing. The psychology of the entrepreneur under capitalism reflects this high responsibility. It is the entrepreneur above all who suffers if the enterprise fails, and it is he who profits first if it is successful. This accounts for the tremendous energy which he puts into his work. His work is governed by no one, but is determined simply by the requirements of the enterprise.

Under socialism the psychology of the economic

organiser is quite different. In this case he is only an official. If he is paid better than the worker—and it is only with difficulty that a state founded on the principle of equality will agree to this—even so this advantage is no stimulus to work. For the risk of the enterprise falls not upon the organiser but upon the state; thus the former loses little in the event of a failure and gains nothing in the event of success. Moreover, the lack of any proper basis for calculation makes it almost impossible to control him. If he has worked conscientiously for six or eight hours in the office he imagines he has done his job. But creative economic activity calls for something more than a formally correct performance of one's duty.

Indeed, many of the failures of our socialist construction are obviously connected with the psychological weaknesses of our organisers. Many millions of pounds of potatoes were received from the peasants and were allowed to spoil; wood was stored only to be stolen, and so on. We may be sure that if a capitalist entrepreneur undertook to deliver potatoes or wood the potatoes would not go rotten and the wood would not be stolen. The entrepreneur will not be indifferent to the loss of the profit for which he is working, and he will vigorously defend himself against any attack upon his capital. At a certain meeting the workers complained that the shoes purchased by the foreign trade commissariat had proved to be unsatisfactory. The representative of the commissariat answered thus: "We are not merchants, proletarians! The American capitalists who supplied the shoes cheated us." The workers accepted this explanation in good humour. But capitalism knows no such good humour, and a merchant who allows himself to be swindled will not hold his position for long. For the capitalist there are no excuses.

But the Soviet official lacks not only the energy and ability necessary for a proper organisation of production but also for the obviously more simple task of preserving the capital in hand. For here too the watchful eye of the manager is necessary—in fact very much so ; and if it is lacking, buildings fall to pieces, ships go down, lathes wear out and material is stolen.

If the work of socialist construction meets with difficulties of a subjective order these difficulties in no way arise from the psychology of the working class but rather from the mentality of the organisers. For the motives with which the socialist society is able to provide them do not correspond to the responsibility they have to bear, or the problems they have to solve. Yet this responsibility is, in view of the tremendous concentration of all economic activity in the hands of the state, literally enormous ; indeed, it is even greater under socialism than under capitalism.

IX

SOCIALISM AND AGRICULTURE

We have proceeded upon the assumption that even before the social revolution—that is to say in the natural course of capitalist evolution—a concentration of all production into large-scale undertakings has taken place and that these undertakings are then nationalised. In the finishing industry there is indeed a strong tendency towards this form of concentration and the consequence is that side by side with it the importance of small-scale industry grows less and less. Nevertheless, the part which small-scale industry plays from an absolute point of view is everywhere still very considerable ; its nationalisation leads, as our own experience shows, to its complete ruin—much to the injury of economic life generally. But if the nationalisation of production, even in the sphere of industry, meets with considerable difficulties, in agriculture these difficulties are simply insuperable. For nothing even comparable to the rapid rate of concentration in industry is to be observed in agriculture. There is only one country in which agriculture is organised upon an almost entirely capitalist basis, namely England ; but the organisation here is the result of an agricultural development which took place in an epoch long passed and in which the conditions were fundamentally different from those ruling to-day. Yet even in England there are still perhaps half a million enterprises. A farm of even a hundred hectares is accounted quite considerable and no tendency towards further concentration can be observed. But on the European continent, and especially in Russia, the dominant organisation is the small-scale farm which relies upon the labour of the peasant and his family. Even in the United States—that country of huge-scale capitalism, of trusts and of millionaires—the small farm, in which hired labour is of subordinate importance, represents the prevailing form of agricultural production. It is true that in actual area the American farms surpass the peasant enterprises of Europe, but this follows from the extensive character of American agriculture.

Economists are still in dispute as to the degree of differentiation within the peasantry; as to whether a process of levelling or a process of further differentiation is taking place. And indeed this controversy has a very considerable bearing upon the question of whether the social revolution can also take root in the rural areas. Communists seek to prove that supporters of the social revolution may be found not only among the few and scattered agricultural labourers but also among the poorest classes of the peasants. It is certainly true that the peasant masses played the most active part in the social revolution; yet we believe that this was the result not of a far-reaching differentiation within the peasantry but rather of the ideas associated with the habits of the *Mir*;[1] in our view the idea of the social revolution will find very much less fertile soil in the villages among the peasant proprietors.

But what interests us chiefly is the effect of social

[1] See also my book, *Agrarentwicklung und Agrarrevolution in Russland*. Osteuropa-Institut in Breslau. Berlin, 1926.

revolution on the land. As to that indeed there can really be no doubt : private property has cast its spell so powerfully upon the poorest peasants, and even to a certain extent upon the agricultural labourers, that the aim of such peasants can only be to extend their possessions at the expense of the large-scale undertakings. The result of social revolution, in the rural areas, can therefore be nothing but the destruction of capitalistically organised agriculture and the complete dispersal of production.

Now what will the socialist state make of all these millions of tiny farms ? How is it to assimilate this vast petty bourgeois population to the planned-economy ? How can it persuade them to combine themselves as rapidly as possible into large-scale collective undertakings ? Even if there were any prospect of such combination taking place, the process would require an enormous time for its completion. But what grounds are there for expecting it to take place ? After all, the agricultural co-operative movement, in spite of all its tremendous development, has so far led nowhere to the growth of collective agricultural enterprises.

The producers co-operative cannot point to any notable successes even in the sphere of industry, in spite of the exertion that has been expended in this direction. Indeed, there is ground for asserting that the origin of the idea of state socialism is connected with the failure of the producers co-operative. Perhaps people think that the producers co-operative will have a better chance of success in agriculture because here even the advantages of large-scale production are questionable ! Or because the co-operative union of agricultural undertakings also demands the union of the peasants' households, a process which involves peculiar difficulties. Any attempt to create collective enterprises on the land artificially could naturally achieve nothing positive.

Thus there remains only one method of assimilating the peasants to the planned-economy ; to regard them as agricultural labourers who live on nationalised land and are bound to do their farming in accordance with the instructions of the state and to deliver up the entire product of their work to the state. But this would leave all the disadvantages of all the small peasant enterprise while abolishing its single advantage—the personal interest of the worker in the result of his labour.

We were not able to persuade ourselves that the socialist state is in a position to organise industry ; but that it can take possession of industry was prophesied by Marx and proved by our own revolution. With agriculture the matter is quite different. The social revolution in the rural areas has nothing to do with socialism ; far from bringing agriculture nearer to the socialist ideal it carries it far in the opposite direction.

If, however, we come to terms with this " petty bourgeois element " then we shall have to give way to its organic demand for a free exchange system ; thus, especially in a predominantly agricultural country, we shall wreck the whole socialist economic system—a system that is, involving a planned distribution of economic goods throughout the entire state.

X

CONCLUSIONS

It is a strange drama that is taking place before us. Socialists, convinced socialists, who look upon life and dogma as one and who will stop at nothing in order to bring about the triumph of their idea—these socialists are destroying with their own hands the fruits of their own creative effort. They are replacing an ostensibly harmonious social order in which exploitation is unknown with an anarchistic order founded upon exploitation—and they hope by this means to increase the resources of the republic and to improve the position of the workers. We see the socialists attempting to attract foreign capital in order that it may build up in our own country that surplus value which at first they felt they were called upon to get rid of.

How are we to explain this strange phenomenon? The right wing socialists will reply as follows: "There is nothing remarkable about it. We foresaw this unhappy result. Marx said that the socialist revolution could only look for success where all the necessary conditions for the introduction of socialism existed; but in Russia, the country of the peasant farmer, these conditions were absent."

It is, of course, possible to find support for this view in various quotations from the works of Marx; yet it is hardly in accordance with the whole spirit of Marxian doctrine.

It is true that industrial capitalism was only indifferently developed in Russia and that it employed only an inconsiderable part of the population. But so far as it did exist, Russian industry was already ripe for a social revolution in the Marxian sense. Owing to the fact that Russian industry was not developing organically to the same extent as was the industry of Western Europe, but that it had been nursed for the last two centuries by the government, by the nobility and by foreign capital—thanks to this fact it had attained an astonishing degree of concentration. This concentration was both horizontal and vertical, that is to say, in the sense of a combination of all stages of one process of production and of its auxiliary processes into a single enterprise. Russia's heavy industry—the works of Putilow, Obuchow, Malzew or those in Brjansk, and the plants of the Russian textile industry are great enterprises not only according to Russian but also according to international standards. Cartellisation and trustification had already gone very far before the revolution began. The large Russian cities represented enormous accumulations of the industrial proletariat and the proletariat found its organisation in the bosom of these great enterprises. The absence of a democratic régime and the impossibility of guaranteeing its economic interests nourished the warlike spirit of the working class and prepared the way for social revolution. The concentration of industry meant an accumulation of wealth with a narrow section of the richer *bourgeoisie*. Moreover, just because the development of Russian industry was, as we have said, inorganic in character, there was wanting in Russia that extensive petty bourgeois class which in European towns stands between the proletariat and the wealthier classes and softens the contrast. And finally, the contrast between the luxury of the leaders of Russian society and the poverty of the poorer classes was more striking in the Russian towns than anywhere else. Altogether the Russian town was quite ripe for the " collapse " which had been prophesied by scientific socialism.

Now the socialists of the right wing will certainly reply that even if this question is open to discussion—the question, that is, whether the Russian town was or was not ripe for the social revolution prophesied by Marx—even so, the social economic aspect of the Russian village at any rate would not fall in with Marx's scheme. And if the Russian village is not yet ready for the social revolution, then Russia as a whole cannot be ready—for Russia is an agricultural country *par excellence*. But if Russia's readiness for socialism is to be measured by the development of the Russian village, then how will the socialists of the right wing answer this question: assuming so literal an interpretation of the Marxian doctrine, will a country like Russia ever be ready for socialism at all? There are, after all, certain limits to industrialisation; the world has grown too small even for countries like England and Germany, which have a much smaller population than Russia. But Russian industry, so far as we can see into the future, will have to depend almost exclusively on the internal market and Russia, which comprises a sixth of the continental world, will have to remain an agricultural country. In Russian agriculture, however, no tangible evidence of concentration has appeared. Thus if one is going to stick to the letter of Marxian doctrine one will have to admit that neither Russia nor any other agricultural country will be ready for the social revolution within measurable time;

in other words, that the theory of scientific socialism cannot be applied to agricultural countries at all. The general validity of Marx's scheme is denied.

In our view it is socialists of the left rather than of the right who represent the true spirit of revolutionary Marxism. It is only among left wing socialists that theory and practice do not part company. If socialism brings happiness, then it must be made, not dreamt. The creative forces of the new order will emerge and transform the world, even if the reality of to-day is not yet appropriate in all its parts to the scheme of development which has been introduced. Even the greatest genius cannot foresee human development in all its many-sidedness. The fact that the social revolution is possible, the fact that the proletariat possesses the power to accomplish such a revolution—these facts prove, according to Marxian doctrine, that " the time has come " ; for the political power of a social class rests, according to Marx, upon economic presuppositions. Thus and only thus, in our view, can the true supporters of the Marxian doctrine argue. It is not for nothing that Mehring, the most eminent representative of scientific socialism in Western Europe, gave his blessing to the Russian revolution.

Yet how comes it that this revolution which, beginning in the town, dragged in the villages as well, which vanquished the counter-revolution so brilliantly, and which was successful in foreign policy—how comes it that this revolution finally proved so unfortunate in the matter of economic construction ? [1]

Officially it is explained that the capitalist stronghold was overcome by too impetuous an attack.

[1] In the three following paragraphs the author enters the lists against Lenin. The first two of these were suppressed by the censor.

Port Arthur, it is said, must be overcome by a slow systematic siege. So that to-day the fortress must be evacuated again in order that trenches may be dug around it once more and a new systematic siege commenced. Now the present writer is admittedly no strategist, but of one thing he is certain : a fortress has never yet been surrendered by its conquerors because it was not captured *according to the rules.* Victors are not sent to judgment, for the capture of a fortress always justifies the methods by which it was taken.

But perhaps we are to understand by the word " fortress " world capitalism, which, after all, is still holding its own. Contrary to the current view we do not hold that successful socialist construction in Russia necessarily presupposes a world revolution. If we were considering so definitely an industrial country as England it would indeed be difficult to conceive of a social revolution unless such a revolution took place throughout the whole civilised world or at least throughout the British colonies. The existence of England without foreign trade is unthinkable, and foreign trade would be utterly destroyed if entirely different legal standards remained in force in those countries with which such trade was carried on. If British foreign trade vanished altogether England would succumb to famine in the first year of the social revolution. Thus, contrary to the prevailing view, the construction of socialism must be attempted not in countries with a high but one-sided industrial development, but in countries which could to a certain extent exist in economic autarchy. Among such countries the United States comes first, and it is followed by Russia.

Is our economic life so far dependent upon Europe that all our want and distress was due entirely to the blockade? Are we not ourselves solely to blame, in that we have not understood how to put our economic system in order? The means of subsistence we have always had in abundance. We exported huge quantities of certain textile raw materials (flax, hemp) and what we lacked of others (cotton, wool) could easily have been made good by expanding our own production. We possess enormous forests and naphtha deposits; we are thus in a position to make good our lack of coal with these two fuels and with peat. We are rich in ores, and rails and locomotives were produced in our factories. There were certain intricate machines which we did not manufacture, yet if socialism were really a higher form of production, then these slight deficiencies would soon be made good out of our own resources. When people suggest that Russia is starving as a result of the blockade, then we cannot help thinking of the English proverb: "Carrying coals to Newcastle." It is precisely in Russia, a country of almost complete economic autarchy, in which the attempt to create socialism should have had the greatest chance of success. We know, however, that reality has given the lie to these hopes, based as they were upon the doctrine of Marxism. No single branch of economic life can be mentioned as having blossomed and borne fruit under the new economic régime, and it was just this complete evidence of failure that compelled even convinced communists to put their hopes henceforth in a partial return to a free exchange of goods and to capitalism. Thus the explanations given both by left and right wing socialists seem to us equally untenable. The true explanation of this failure to construct a socialist economic system is provided, we believe, in the foregoing pages.

From the point of view of socialist theory, the different elements of Russian economic life were not equally ready for socialist reconstruction. But if the reconstruction that was actually attempted continually degenerated—by the confession of our communists—into a " serial story of catastrophies ", while the renunciation of socialism under the New Economic Policy led almost without exception to an improvement of the situation, then it is clear that the wreck of socialist economic construction cannot only be explained by the unsuitability of the time and place. On the contrary, Russian experience bears out in the clearest manner our basic conclusion—namely, that the principle of socialism is not creative ; that it leads the economic life of society not to fruition but to ruin.

PART II
THE RESULTS OF ECONOMIC PLANNING IN RUSSIA
(1934)

PREFACE

My essay on the *Doctrines of Marxism in the Light of the Russian Revolution* was based upon experiences gained during the early years of socialist construction in Russia, which ended abruptly with the advent of the N.E.P. in March 1921. It soon became evident that the task of constructing a socialist state in Soviet Russia had not been definitely abandoned when this change took place. After many years of experiment the new schemes for socialist construction took form in the far-reaching Five Year Plan, which for a time kept the whole world in a state of suspense. The fundamental difference between this second scheme and the first lay in the fact that it was planned on the lines of a money economy and not on natural socialism.

The main object of the present essay is to inquire into Russia's economic development under the Five Year Plan. Now, this plan did not emerge suddenly but was the outcome of eleven years of preparation, a general outline of which period is here set forth.

It is no concrete description of Russian economic events that we propose to give. We shall examine them from a theoretical standpoint. And as the basic theoretical problems have been explained in the foregoing essay, we can confine ourselves here to concise theoretical observations and a description of the general economic development. Whereas the problem of natural socialism formed the main point of the first essay, the present one deals predominantly with the development of economic planning on a monetary basis.

I

THE BEGINNINGS OF THE COMMUNIST "PLANNED ECONOMY"

A. The Attempt at State-Capitalism

The Five Year Plan was the final outcome of the communist planned economy. It did not emerge suddenly, but was rather the result of eleven years of development. Of this development we propose here to give a brief account.

Lenin, the leader of the Russian Revolution, was an orthodox Marxist, and as such he was little concerned, before he seized power, as to how the economic system would have to be developed after the victory of the social revolution. He sought to placate his adherents with the assurance that no especial difficulties were to be expected here.[1]

But after the October revolution he immediately realised that the task of building up Communism was by no means so easy as he had thought, and he sought to

[1] In his well-known treatise, *State and Revolution*, written at the time of his flight from Petrograd after the July revolution—and on the eve of the October one—Lenin expresses the conviction that, at the commencement of a socialist régime, the control of production and distribution and the registration of labour and commodities must be put into the hands of an armed proletariat. " Capitalism," he says, " has so enormously simplified the methods of control and registration that they present no

simplify it so far as possible. His aim was to retain the existing capitalist organisation with its valuable managerial personnel, placing it under the control partly of the Soviet Government and partly of the workers themselves (syndicalistic tendencies). At that time his slogan was :[1] "Under a Soviet government State-Capitalism constitutes three-quarters of Socialism." He would not countenance the efforts of his comrades to nationalise everything as quickly as possible. But, in accordance with the ideas developed by Rudolf Hilferding in his well-known book, *Financial Capital*, Lenin had the banks nationalised as early as the 14th December, 1917 ; he hoped that in this way the Soviet Government might gain control of the entire capitalist economic system without destroying its internal organisation.

This attempt at State-Capitalism failed utterly. It was finally abandoned in the summer of 1918, barely nine months later, and the Soviet Government introduced an entirely new economic policy. Officially it was explained that it was impossible to leave the large-scale undertakings in the hands of the capitalists when civil war broke out, at a time when it was necessary to do battle with the spiritual friends of these same capitalists at the fronts.

This explanation is not without weight, but it is not the whole explanation. There was another and deeper reason for the failure of the attempt. The communist

difficulties to those who can read and write. The ability to observe and record and to make out receipts—this, with a knowledge of the four rules of arithmetic, is all that is required. (Russian edition, *Moskovsky Rabocy*, 1923, p. 91. The work has been translated into all languages.)

[1] *Lenin's Collected Works* (Russian), vol. xxiii, p. 484.

party won power by exciting and inflaming all the anarchist passions of the masses. Lenin's well-known slogan ran as follows: "Rob the robber." Property was no longer secure, nor even were the lives of the property-owners. When Lenin, having come to his senses, sought to create order, he was faced with an extraordinarily difficult task. The government had lost much of its power; the principle, "All power to the local Soviets," held sway ("Vlast' na mestach!"). The October revolution was no less than a social revolution: the bourgeois society was struck to the heart—it was dead. Lenin as an adherent of historical materialism, was deceived by the fact that the framework of the economic system remained standing and that the wheels of the economic machine, in obedience to the law of inertia, were still turning—though ever more slowly. He did not realise that certain legal principles constitute the very essence of the bourgeois society, and that in the moment when these principles are repudiated, either by a popular movement or by a new government, the bourgeois society ceases to exist. He thought he could nationalise the banks. In reality he only seized their buildings, safes, accounts and books; but the banks, as banks, the very flower of the bourgeois order, had ceased to exist two months after the communist revolution. It was because bourgeois society lay shattered that State-Capitalism could not be accomplished. Now it remained to build up a new economic order on the ruins of the old.

B. "War-communism"

The period which began in the summer of 1918 and came to an end barely three years later in March 1921, is usually described as the period of " War-communism ". The communists only applied this description to it subsequently. They wanted to explain that this system was forced upon them by war, and that they would not accept responsibility for it. There is no doubt that the economic administration at this time was extremely pressed for war material. In war the demands of war take precedence over all others. War exhausts the economic system, and a situation of such gravity may arise that it is necessary, in order to satisfy the elementary needs of the people, to distribute goods in accordance with communist principles. In all the countries which took part in the World War certain communistic tendencies appeared. In Soviet Russia, where the foreign war was followed by a civil war which raged for over two years, and which brought more devastation in its wake than the bitterest conflict with alien powers, communist tendencies were all the more strongly in evidence.

And yet this interpretation of the economic development of this period does not tell the whole truth. The measures which were taken at that time were not thought of as temporary. Indeed, many economic institutions which came into existence then outlasted the period and form, even to-day, the backbone of the Soviet economic system. The aim of the economic policy of the Soviet Government was not only to adapt economic life to the needs of war, but also to erect on the foundation of this war-economy a logical system of " natural " socialism. Twice in this period the war subsided; first in the winter of 1920 after the victory of the Soviets over Kolčak and Denikin and for a second time after the final overthrow of the counter-revolution in November

1920 ; but in these comparatively peaceful periods there were no changes in the economic system. On the contrary, communism indulged in what may be called its greatest orgies in the months preceding the announcement of the New Economic Policy. The sudden abandonment of the methods of War-communism was not undertaken voluntarily ; it was absolutely unavoidable, owing to the development of a political situation which endangered Soviet power.

The concentration of dictatorial power with the political bureau of the party (Politbureau), which had taken place in the civil war, formed the political foundation for the attempt to bring about a logical system of " natural " socialism. The syndicalistic tendencies which appeared immediately after the October rebellion in the form of the so-called Workers' Control and which soon fell into a state of chaos, were completely abandoned. The aims of the economic administration are clearly expressed in the following resolution which was drawn up at the conference of Economic Councils in January 1920, in accordance with Lenin's proposal : [1] " The centralisation of the national economic administration is the principal means at the disposal of the victorious proletariat for developing the productive forces of the country and for securing to industry a leading part in economic life." The supreme direction of the economic system lay at first in the hands of the Supreme Economic Council (Russian abbreviation : W.S.N.Ch.). This organisation, however, later

[1] *Fifteen Years of Soviet Construction, 1917–1932*. A collection of articles edited by Pasukanis. State publishing department, 1932. Article by G. Amfiteatrov and L. Ginzburg : " The principal stages in the development of organisation forms in the socialist economy and of Soviet law," p. 324.

confined itself to the management of industry, and the supreme direction of the economic system was finally taken over by the Labour and Defence Council (S.T.O.) in 1920. " The S.T.O. determines the general economic plan of the R.S.F.S.R., submits it to the All-Russian Executive Committee for ratification, directs in accordance with this plan the work of the economic people's commissariats, superintends the execution of the plan, and makes, when necessary, exceptions to it." [1] Accordingly the Soviet Government sought to bring all production, without exception, under its control. Here it met with insuperable difficulties in the sphere of agriculture. As a result of the agrarian revolution, agriculture was entirely broken up into peasant holdings ; and it was now extraordinarily difficult, for political as well as economic reasons, to bring it under the control of the Soviet Government. The latter had mainly to content itself with expropriating the surpluses of agricultural products. It is true that the VIIIth Soviet Congress of December 1920 decided to set up seed committees (Posevkomy) which should be free to dispose of the stock and seeds of the peasants, and which would prescribe sowing plans for them. Owing, however, to the early change in economic policy, there was not time for any serious attempt to carry out this project.

Market transactions were to be entirely suspended, and there was to be no " horizontal " movement of goods whatever ; all goods were to be put at the disposal of the central authorities and distributed by them. Such movement of goods was to take place without money.

[1] Resolutions of the Eighth U.S.S.R. Congress. Shorthand report, 1921, p. 281.

At that time Lenin thought that money was [1] " a testimony of the right of the exploiter to obtain social goods with a view to speculation, profit, and plundering the workers ". Money issues were not restricted, as no one cared about the depreciation of money. Relations between the state undertakings were to be regulated without money. Wages consisted mainly of rations in kind. Taxes were not paid, and the municipalities performed their services free of charge.

Nevertheless, the Soviet Government did feel the need of bringing goods to a common denominator. At the end of 1920 state enterprises were instructed to reckon in units of labour value. No one, however, took this official decision seriously.

The system of natural socialism was developed logically by the Soviet Government ; but it would not function, and had to be supplemented by a very restricted market business. Nationalised production and distribution were almost paralysed. That involved catastrophe, at first for the towns, which were literally deserted, and then for the country. When the Soviet Government sought to complete the development of this system, immediately after the end of the war, it met with desperate resistance from all sections of the community. At that time such a resistance was still possible, for the Soviet power was not yet so complete, and the masses not yet so disorganised, discouraged and disarmed as later. A situation had arisen which imperilled Soviet power, and Lenin resolved, contrary to the wishes of his closest friends, to change the course as quickly as possible.

[1] *Lenin's Collected Works*, 3rd edition, vol. xxiv, p. 103 (Russian).

Communists prefer not to discuss the causes of this failure. Observers usually imagine that it is to be explained by the fact that the Russian economic system was not ripe for socialism because it was not sufficiently concentrated. This explanation cannot be accepted, for it is in contradiction to the facts. If the success of an attempt to introduce natural socialism depended only on production being to a high degree centralised, then the Russian large-scale industry actually provided excellent material for such an attempt; for although the industry in question was not, taken as a whole, of any great extent, it was concentrated in very big undertakings. Thus, the creation of a socialist administration for an industry of this type should have been a comparatively simple task. Its management was taken over by the Supreme Economic Council, within which were constituted Governing Boards (Glavki) for each branch of industry (at the end of this period there were more than forty of these). One might well believe that the Soviet Government would be successful in its development of large-scale industry, for this department of the economic system was, after all, most ripe for socialisation. Yet in reality it was precisely in this sphere that the collapse was most appalling. In 1920 production is said to have fallen to 13 per cent of that of the pre-war period.[1] The cause of this decline was not only the war, but also, to a large extent, the utterly defective distribution of the means of production under the system of natural socialism.

Under capitalism each undertaking obtains the means

The Five Year Plan of Economic Construction in the U.S.S.R. (*Planovoe Chozyaystvo*, Moscow, 1929, vol. i, p. 15).

of production independently on the market, and its potentialities in this respect correspond to its output. Under natural socialism the conditions for the provision of the means of production are quite different. The products of each undertaking are put at the disposal of a corresponding Governing Board, without being brought to a common denominator ; it then remains for the management of the undertaking to apply to a whole series of Governing Boards for the necessary means of production. It is quite impossible for the Governing Boards to assess the output of the undertaking, and indeed this is hardly taken into account ; of far greater significance is the political importance of the management. Every Governing Board is swayed by its own considerations, according to which it distributes the means of production, and the latter are not checked up one with another.

The Governing Boards ought to have known, with regard to the whole country, exactly where the means of production were to be found, and in what quantity and quality ; but they did not know, and their orders were often entirely erroneous. On the other hand the director of an undertaking might have all the necessary means of production at hand, yet would have to remain a passive observer ; for he was only able to make use of those means of production which were allotted to him by the Governing Boards.

It almost never happened that the production goods allotted to an undertaking by various Governing Boards were matched in quantity or quality. As the means of production are complementary the whole of industry was in this way gradually paralysed, although the country still possessed considerable stocks of unused production goods. From time to time it was announced that certain undertakings were to have precedence—this applied to industries supplying war-material—so that those which were not favoured suffered all the more. This catastrophic situation was so obviously connected with the activities of the Governing Boards (Glavki) that the very name came to be hated. Later, when analogous institutions came into existence, no one dared to describe them in this way.[1]

Thus we see that the economic system suffered from defects which had nothing to do with the war; they were inherent defects of natural socialism—defects which have been demonstrated in the first section of the present volume. For that reason no improvement in the condition of industry could be traced in the four months which followed the conclusion of the war. The system brought misery and decay to the towns; while agri-

[1] For details of the distribution of producers' goods during War-communism, see L. Krizman, *The Heroic Age of the Russian Revolution.* An analytical essay on so-called War-communism, 2nd Edition. State publishing department, 1926, pp. 120–5 (Russian). Trans. into German.

See also the article on *Fifteen Years of Soviet Construction*, *op. cit.*, pp. 337–8. Krizman, who, as the title of his book shows, is a great admirer of War-communism, traces a certain analogy between capitalist and communist systems in respect of their development by means of a succession of crises. "Bound up with these anarchic features of a proletarian natural socialism," he writes (p. 125), "is the difficulty of maintaining supplies, a problem every bit as acute as the question of markets in a capitalist trading system. In the latter, there are periods of stagnation and crisis alternating with periods of great prosperity; in the former, one crisis follows another, and from time to time localised troubles are fermented into a general situation of great difficulty." But the author does not quite grasp the difference between the two systems. The capitalist economy enjoys periods of great prosperity which ensure the vitality of the system; natural socialism drifts from one depression to another, and accordingly lacks the vitality necessary to its existence.

culture was ruined in its turn by the civil war, the agrarian revolution and the confiscations of surpluses. Thus there came about the appalling famine of 1921–2, which the announcement of the New Economic Policy could no longer prevent.[1]

C. The New Economic Policy

The essence of the change involved by the New Economic Policy (Russian abbrev. N.E.P.) was the restoration of the market—i.e. of a horizontal connection between separate enterprises. This had formerly been forbidden in favour of one all-embracing socialist enterprise. At the same time the co-operation of private business was to be permitted. While the period of War-communism gave a negative testimony in favour of the Market Economy, the period of the New Economic Policy gave a positive proof of its advantages. In spite of the famine and of the still primitive organisation of the market, signs of revival could be observed immediately the New Economic Policy was announced. The populations of the areas which had been spared harvest failure took up their work with renewed hope. The wheels of industry, which had been brought to a standstill, picked up slowly at first, but with the end of the famine in the autumn of 1922 a more rapid process of economic reconstruction set in. All this made an impression on the communists. The Soviet Government sought to restore certain institutions of the capitalist society.

[1] For details of agricultural development under War-communism, see my *Agrarentwicklung und Agrarrevolution in Russland*, Osteuropa-Institut in Breslau, *Quellen und Studien, Abteilung Wirtschaft*, vol. ii, Berlin, 1925, pt. 2, pp. 137–78.

Among observers this fact led to the erroneous view that the problem of building up a socialist economy was settled. In fact it was far from settled.

As early as March 1922, a year after the announcement of the New Economic Policy, Lenin declared that the retreat of socialism must be suspended and that it must entrench itself on the commanding positions of economic life—i.e. in its centralised sections. In the hands of the Soviet Government there still remained the large-scale industry, transport, the reconstructed credit system and foreign trade. The government had also established trading organisations, particularly with a view to obtaining supplies of agricultural products. The co-operative societies had been restored, and they too remained under the management of the Soviet state, merely constituting a specific form of state enterprise.

All these organisations adopted certain forms of capitalistic organisation. But no decisive significance should be ascribed to this fact. The nationalised undertakings performed certain tasks which were set them by the communist state and their work was determined not with a view to making the greatest possible profit, but principally in the interests of politics. The independence of these undertakings remained very limited. Internally they exhibited bureaucratic rather than capitalistic characteristics. It was on this ground that Lenin referred to the state undertakings as socialistic, and contrasted the socialist sector of society with the private.[1] Both sectors

[1] Foreign observers usually describe state undertakings as " state-capitalist " and, correspondingly, the whole Soviet economy under the Five Year Plan as state-capitalism. We consider these labels to be misleading, for profit-making is by no means the mainspring of the Soviet system. The reason why foreigners are unwilling to apply the term socialism to Russian state undertakings is that, unlike the Russians, they

found their formally free connection (" smyčka ", according to Lenin) on the market. The whole system of the New Economic Policy was considered by Lenin as a serious long-run proposition. In his view the future of Soviet economic life depended on whether the socialist sector would subordinate itself to the private, or the private to the socialist.

Although the situation of the small private enterprises was by no means favourable in the face of competition from the large-scale and in every respect privileged state undertakings, they nevertheless showed great vitality. Private business was always ready to pay much higher prices to agriculture and large-scale industry than were the state trading organisations; moreover, small-scale industry competed very successfully with large-scale for materials. The weakness of the private sector was legal, not economic, and this fact later sealed its fate.

Owing to the fact that in the economic sphere, Lenin had changed his course with all possible speed, it was possible for him to refuse to make concessions in the political sphere. The omnipotence of the party leaders which came into existence during the civil war, and for

have had none of the bitter experiences of natural socialism in their own countries and still prefer to think of socialism as a " natural " system of economy. And because, since the introduction of the N.E.P., the Russian system is still run on a money basis, they fail to see how it can be called socialism.

But there is another interesting psychological reason why the foreign observer, though admitting that a socialist system is under construction in Soviet Russia, will never see that it is already there. For the average European, good bourgeois politician as he may be at home, still thinks of socialism as the embodiment of all that is good in the social system. And since it is obvious that the life of a Russian bourgeois is not lived on a bed of roses, it can only be that the structure is not yet complete—in fact that there is still a relic of wicked capitalism in Soviet Russia.

which the system of the Soviets served merely as a cloak, remained unscathed. In this omnipotence, according to Lenin, was realised the " Dictatorship of the Proletariat ", an institution which he usually defined in some such way as this : it was a power which " knows no limits, which is restricted by no laws and absolutely no regulation, and which rests on might alone ".[1] When governmental power was of this nature, an ability to compete in economic life could have no decisive bearing upon the future of private enterprises. Even when a Civil Code—which could be very elastically interpreted —was published at the end of 1922, private business remained without protection against the all-powerful communist authorities. It was from that direction that the N.E.P. system was imperilled : its collapse came sooner than Lenin expected.

By the end of 1923, two and a half years after the New Economic Policy was announced, it was clear that private business possessed no legal security. Within the party an opposition movement developed, at the head of which stood Trotsky ; at that time, after Lenin had fallen ill, he was the leading spirit in the party. Trotsky recognised the economic progress which had taken place under the New Economic Policy. He believed, however, that it threatened the future of socialism. He pointed out that the influence of the peasantry was growing, and that a class of large-scale peasants was coming into existence which would endanger Soviet power. The peasantry ought therefore to be subjected to heavier pressure. This point of view was in contradiction to the idea of an alliance between workers and peasants, upon which, according to Lenin's promises, the immediate

[1] *Lenin's Collected Works*, 1st Edition, vol. vii, p. 124.

future of the Soviet state was to be founded. The opposition was suppressed and Trotsky was silenced. Nevertheless, his agitation remained not without influence upon party politics. At the beginning of 1924, the greater part of the private capital which had accumulated in the three years since the announcement of the New Economic Policy, was seized. Private trade was prevented from distributing the products of large-scale industry and its place was taken by the co-operative societies which, though unwieldy, were under the control of the Soviet Government. Certain measures were also taken against the well-to-do peasants.

Nevertheless the pro-peasant feeling in the party was not by this means finally overcome. In May 1925, at the Union Conference of the Soviets, liberal policy celebrated its greatest victories so far as the peasantry was concerned. It was thought that the peasant would dispose of his crops to the government at the lowest prices and it was even sought to reconcile the well-to-do peasants. Then it was that Bucharin, the theoretician of communism, exclaimed " enrichissez-vous ". As the opposition ironically expressed it later, at that time one believed in the peaceful assimilation of the Kulaks (well-to-do peasants) by socialism.

The " commanding positions " of economic life were to form the foundation of the socialist structure. Since the state undertakings were not capitalistic, they could not be conducted without a plan. As monopolistic organisations they tended to demand very high prices for their products. But as the managements were not interested in the profitability of their undertakings, they also had no special reasons for seeking a reduction of costs. To what results such an attitude can lead was shown by the one serious over-production crisis which occurred in large-scale industry at the beginning of 1924—at a time when its production was barely a third of that of the pre-war period. One cause of this crisis was that the peasants had suffered severe losses in the inflation of autumn 1923. By finally stabilising the currency in February 1924, the Soviet Government had removed this cause of the slump. But there remained another cause ; the enormously high prices of industrial goods. Thus in October 1923 the wholesale index for industrial goods reached 2,757 (the one for 1913 being 1,000), while the wholesale index for agricultural products was at that time only 888. The ratio of the two indices was therefore 3 to 10. Such being the state of affairs, the peasant sought to deal not with large-scale industry, but with small private concerns ; or, where the latter could not supply the necessary goods, his husbandry remained autarchic. It was not to be expected that unwieldy, nationalised industry would lower its prices to any considerable extent. The Soviet Government had to intervene. And it did succeed, from the 1st April, 1924 to the 1st July, 1925, in lowering prices of industrial goods by 31·2 per cent.[1] The Soviet Government hoped that by quickly increasing production their costs would be correspondingly lowered, and here also its hope was to a large extent fulfilled. This and analogous episodes have clearly proved that the monopolistic state undertakings are not in a position, without guidance from above, to perform their economic work. The government has to supervise them, it has to determine selling prices and so compel them to reduce production costs.

[1] *Ten Years of Internal Trade in the U.S.S.R.* (Narkomtorg, 1928, p. 79).

While the bourgeois governments confine themselves to planning their budgets, the Soviet Government had become accustomed to sanctioning numerous plans for the most important branches of industry—i.e. for large-scale industry, for transport, for foreign trade, for the acquisition of agricultural products and so on. The State Planning Commission (Russian abbrev., Gosplan) which was set up under the Labour and Defence Council (S.T.O.) in February 1921—on the eve of the announcement of the New Economic Policy—busied itself with the elaboration of these plans. Thus, of necessity, there soon arose the idea of a General Economic Plan, without which the various individual plans might come into conflict with one another.

The New Economic Policy, therefore, in no way disposed of the problem of the General Economic Plan. On the contrary, it created the conditions in which the problem might more than ever be put on the party agenda. In the period of War-communism a good deal was said of a General Plan, but no serious attempt was made to work one out. The reason for this was that the elaboration of a well-considered economic plan demands, as first essential, a proper balance sheet in terms of money. The idea of a general plan in an economic system without money involves an inner contradiction; it is impossible to gain any clear view of such a system, and it is therefore impossible to make a plan for it. In the three years which followed the announcement of the New Economic Policy there could be no general plan simply because there was no stable money. Only after the currency had been put in order in February 1924 did the problem of a General Economic Plan become a real one. In the summer of 1925, the State

Planning Commission published for the first time the outline of a General Economic Plan ; the title was *The Economic Control-figures of the U.S.S.R. for the year 1925–6* (at that time the economic year was reckoned from October 1st to September 30th). This event was of decisive significance in the further development of the Soviet Economy.

The State Planning Commission, in which at that time non-party experts played the leading part, proposed for itself a modest aim. The control-figures were not to replace the plans of the individual departments, but the latter were to take the control-figures into account when elaborating their own plans, in order to avoid coming into conflict with the general line of development. The principal purpose of the control-figures was to forecast the development of private trade—especially of large-scale peasant agriculture—the progress of which the Gosplan had no wish to interrupt. From this forecast the administrations of nationalised undertakings obtained directives, which however they were not to obey mechanically, but were to adapt to the conditions of the market. To maintain the equilibrium of supply and demand on the market and to preserve the free connection on the market of the private and socialist sectors of society—this was regarded by the Gosplan as the most important task of the economic administration.

Nevertheless, the Gosplan was subjected to pressure from the ruling party. The aim of the latter was the rapid reconstruction and expansion of industry. The means to this end were to be supplied by the peasantry. The peasants were to supply, abundantly and cheaply, food for the industrial workers and raw materials for the factories ; in addition they were to provide a surplus of their products, particularly of grain, for export purposes, since a considerable import of machinery and of raw material was necessary for the reconstruction of industry. Here the planning commission, basing its judgment on the experiences of 1923–4, when prices had not yet been stabilised, was far too optimistic as to the possibility of procuring grain cheaply. In 1923–4, the Soviet Government was able to purchase from the peasants, at prices two or three times lower than before the war, enough grain to make possible an export of 2·7 million tons at a good profit after the requirements of the still modest internal market had been fully satisfied. In 1924–5, it is true, the government was unable to repeat its cheap grain purchases and achieve a considerable export as it had hoped to do ; this however was regarded as accidental and ascribed to the bad harvest of 1924. In 1925 an excellent harvest was expected and the Gosplan hoped that a situation similar to that of 1923–4 would develop on the grain market. The state trading organisations got ready, in *viribus unitis*, to buy up grain from the peasants at prices lower than before the war.

On account of the very considerable progress which free trading had made in the meantime, these hopes were not fulfilled. The trading organisations were compelled to buy up grain at somewhat higher prices than those ruling before the war (index 118·9, 1913 = 100).[1] Instead of 13 million tons, as was planned, it was only possible to buy 9·6 million, and instead of 5 to 6 million tons, only 2·1 million were exported—that is, less than in 1923–4. Although the powerful state organisations exerted

[1] *Economic Bulletin of the Institute of Economic Research*, November-December, 1927, p. 54.

pressure on the grain market, their monopoly control was not such that they were able to dictate prices to the peasants. Even at such prices the peasant received something like 40 per cent less than before the war, in terms of industrial goods.[1]

The partial failure on the grain market created difficulties for the Soviet Government. Once more the left opposition in the party gathered strength. The whole of Lenin's old guard, the intellectuals, came to terms with Trotsky. The opposition was crushed by Stalin, the General Secretary of the party, who was bringing the organisation more and more under his sole control; later on, in December 1927, the leader of the opposition was turned out of the party by the 15th party congress. But gradually Stalin made the opposition programme his own.

The partial failure of the economic plan for 1925–6 could not shake the party's faith in a planned economy. It did not even come to the conclusion that the plans should be more cautiously drawn up, or that such enormous demands should not be made upon the peasants. The control-figures appeared annually since the summer of 1925. They are worked out with increasing care, so that for the years 1927–8 and 1928–9 (the first year of Five Year Plan period) they form the most important evidence of the character of Soviet economics. The binding significance of the control-figures for the economic administration is emphasised more and more, and the sanctioning of the plans of individual branches of industry is finally given up. After the rapid reconstruction of the older industry had taken place, the principal aim of the planned economy

[1] *Ten Years of Internal Trade*, pp. 108–10.

was declared to be the creation of a new heavy industry. Nevertheless, the authors of the control-figures still attempted to maintain the formally free connection between the private and socialist sectors of society; they still believed that the most important task of economic planning was to preserve the equilibrium of supply and demand on the market.

The efforts of the planning commission were in vain; the demands made upon the peasants were far too great to be met, and the Soviet Government, for its part, was not concerned to spare business done on the free market. It realised that as long as private trade existed, prices "according to plan" could not be enforced; therefore it decided to eliminate private trade. First of all, by means of administrative measures, it eliminated private capital from the interregional grain trade, and then it sought to drive the private trader from all departments of business by means of arbitrary taxation and confiscation. Further, most of the small-scale industrial enterprises which competed with large-scale industry for raw material were closed down on one pretext or another. In so far as the Soviet Government was thus enabled to enforce predetermined purchase prices, these measures achieved their purpose. The price index of grain purchased by the state trading organisations fell from 118·9 in 1925–6 to 105·8 in 1926–7. But at the same time the market lost much of its attraction for the peasant. Although the reconstruction of grain-growing areas continued at an increasing pace up to and including 1926, and although the harvest for 1926 turned out very well, the percentage of grain brought to the market in the years 1924–5, 1925–6 and 1926–7 fluctuated between 14 and 15 per cent, while before the war it had reached

22·8 per cent [1]; thus no progress could be detected. The peasants stored their grain or fed it to the animals; private trade still played an important part on the market for animal products, and the state organisations had to pay correspondingly high prices for them (index = 163·1). In 1926–7 only $2\frac{1}{4}$ million tons of grain were exported, again less than in 1923–4.

The extensive investments into industry, amounting to nearly a milliard roubles, and the increase in the circulation of money by 25 per cent (from 1343·3 mill. roubles on October 1st, 1925 to 1670·8 mill. on October 1st, 1927; before the war the circulation over a greater territory was 1·7 milliard roubles) led the Soviet state into a condition of inflation—though as yet mild. Together with the regulation of prices and the relatively high wages of the workers—in 1926–7 the pre-war wage-rates were surpassed—this condition of inflation resulted in the rural areas being inadequately provided with industrial goods, and in the peasants being increasingly reluctant to dispose of their products. The Soviet Government, on its part, was tempted to expropriate these products forcibly.

In its review of economic development in the year 1926–7, the Institute for Economic Research gave warning of this danger. "Any attempt to overcome the discrepancies of the market in a combined commodity and money economy by non-economic methods," writes the Institute,[2] "must lead, in its logical development,

[1] *Economic Bulletin of the Institute of Economic Research*, 1927, No. 11–12, p. 52. The last percentage according to: "An inquiry into socialist reconstruction of agriculture." Material for an inquiry into the people's commissariat for the inspection of workers and peasants. Edited by J. A. Jakovlev, 1928, p. 15.

[2] See above, p. 15.

to the economic methods of War-communism, with all its characteristic features."

The Institute also pointed to the recrudescence of certain phenomena which recalled War-communism: the movement of " knapsackcarriers " from the subsidised areas to the south in search of " white flour "; the illicit trade in fixed-price goods; the sale of deficiency goods by the shops, not in the ordinary way of sale to all customers, but according to special standards, such as the production of membership cards of the co-operatives or of the certificates of " responsible workers " (privileged communists); the purchase of certain raw materials with part payment in goods; and so on. " This," the Institute continues, " may lead to a decline in the productive power of the villages and to a severe decrease of the marketable part of agricultural products."

At that time memories of the dreadful years of War-communism were still fresh, and the admonitions of the Institute aroused a storm of indignation in the party. On the strength of this review the Institute was closed down; but its forecast soon proved to have been right.

Events took the course described. In 1927 the ever more violent persecution of the peasants had brought the reconstruction of grain farming almost to a standstill, and at the same time the harvest, after two fortunate years, was indifferent. Owing to the abolition of private business, " trade-deserts " made their appearance in country districts. The peasants were unwilling to sell grain at low prices in order that they might collect paper money which had no one's confidence. Meanwhile the government, having destroyed the private grain trade, assumed the entire responsibility for feeding the populace. Thus in January 1928 a far-reaching decision was forced upon it: it decided to close the markets in the country districts, and to revert to the compulsory expropriation of grain and of certain raw materials. The last pillar of the N.E.P. system had collapsed.

The significance of what had happened was not yet quite clear to the Soviet Government. It regarded it as an isolated phenomenon, and attempted in the spring to revive the free purchase of grain. But as in all other respects the principles of economic policy remained unchanged, it was not possible to obtain large quantities of agricultural products from the peasants at fixed prices. Between the free and the fixed prices there opened up an unbridgeable abyss. The N.E.P. system was dead. The Soviet Government could not turn back; it was confronted by the task of realising the Five Year Plan.

Thus even before the Five Year Plan came into force the first attempts at planning had led to the partial destruction of the private forms of economic life and to the revival of the forcible expropriation of agricultural products. Planned economy was plainly degenerating into an economy of force.

II

THE ESSENCE OF THE FIVE YEAR PLAN

THE development of planning led necessarily to the idea of constructing plans for longer periods than one year. It was thought by this means to achieve greater ends. The first outline of a Five Year Plan was completed as early as March 1927, but the examination of the plan lasted for more than two years, so that only on the 28th May, 1929, at the Union Conference of the Soviets, amidst much rejoicing, was the Five Year Plan for the socialist construction of the U.S.S.R. sanctioned.[1] It was, however, to operate as from the 1st October, 1928, that is to say, for the five years 1928–9, to 1932–3 inclusive; and in working out the control-figures for 1928–9, the plan was taken into account.

At the time when the Five Year Plan was being elaborated there occurred an important change of feeling in the party. The immediate task of building up socialism in a country was finally placed upon the party agenda, and this necessarily influenced the character of the work of planning. Hitherto, the control-figures had been established on a basis of the rate of development in various branches of industry for the preceding years; the future rate of development was forecast by reference to the past. This was described as the "genetical"

[1] *The Five Year Plan of Economic Construction in the U.S.S.R.*, vol. i; vol. ii, parts 1 and 2; vol. iii.

method, or the method of "extrapolation". Although the members of the Gosplan were convinced opponents of a "force" economy, planning had nevertheless destroyed the free interplay of the socialist and private sectors of economic life. The non-party experts regarded the reversion to force as extraordinarily dangerous, and they believed, therefore, that the enactment of the Five Year Plan was inopportune.

But in opposition to the "genetical" school of thought there gradually arose within the Gosplan a "teleological" school. The latter believed itself to represent orthodox communism and as such was supported by the Soviet Government. According to the "teleologists", the Russian proletariat had, with the Social Revolution, already leapt from the bondage of necessity into freedom. Soviet economic life could develop at a pace which was out of the question for capitalism. It was not necessary to pay much attention to the past. They should set themselves a great purpose and then seek the means to accomplish it. The feeling of communist political economists was admirably expressed in the following words of Strumilin, a political economist who played a leading part in the final composition of the Five Year Plan: "The art of Planning", thinks Strumilin,[1] "does not reconcile itself to the existing world. Its aim is not to know this world, but to change it. It creates a new world for itself, actively."

The prudence of the experts was spurned.

> Influenced by the economic difficulties of the time, [says the foreword to the Five Year Plan] [2] many are inclined to

[1] "The Theory of Planning", in *Planovoe Chozyaystvo* (Russian journal), 1928, vol. i, p. 124.

[2] *The Five Year Plan* . . ., vol. i, pp. 6–7.

> question whether this is the appropriate moment to introduce a " long-range " plan. Our opponents refer incessantly to the specific contradiction between the magnitude of our tasks of construction and production, and the character of the present economic difficulties . . . But the conquest of our difficulties, which in themselves must be regarded as halting stages on the road to construction, can only be accomplished by way of an unswerving execution of the plan before us, by means of great works and of socialist offensive on a wide front.

Although the collaboration of the non-party experts was not dispensed with (the complexity of the work made this impossible in the circumstances), heavy pressure was exerted upon them in order to secure a wide extension of the plans.[1] Moreover, the Soviet Congress had not sanctioned the more carefully considered " introductory plan ", but rather the less thought-out " optimal " plan—the latter being based upon a number of unjustifiable assumptions, such as, for example, five years without a harvest failure. In spite of this the Five Year Plan is not to be regarded as the outcome of purely communistic effort ; in outline it was the result of the collaboration of the best Russian minds. Wide use was made of numerous preliminary studies which had been drawn up, even before the war, by the Imperial Russian Technical Association under the direction of the well-

[1] The moral conditions under which Intellectuals were forced to work when drawing up the F.Y.P. may be imagined from these remarks by the communist, Strumilin : " Undoubtedly I could, by bringing the necessary pressure to bear on the experts, reach the point of throwing all caution to the winds. But it would hardly serve any useful purpose to put such a strain on the ' civil ' courage of the said experts, who prefer to advocate the speeding-up of construction in the lobbies rather than to mark time in prison because their tempo has been too slow." (*Planovoe Chozyaystvo*, 1929, vol. i, p. 109.)

known experts on Russian Economic conditions, V. I. Kovalevskij and Professor L. I. Lutugin.

The principal aims of the Five Year Plan had already been proposed in the " control-figures ". Now, however, development was to proceed at an incomparably greater rate. The aims were determined not only by economic, but also, to a large extent, by political considerations. In quantity, if not in quality, Russian large-scale industry had been restored by the beginning of the Five Year Plan (though there had been great changes in its composition). On the other hand, since 1928, a retrograde movement had been perceptible in agriculture under the influence of the coercive methods ; at the beginning of the Five Year Plan it had recovered neither quantitatively nor qualitatively. As the population at the beginning of the Five Year Plan had already increased by about 10 per cent as compared with pre-war times, a dangerous condition was created which ought first of all to have been dealt with. Owing to the severe over-population in the rural districts of central Russia, the idea of industrialisation did not conflict with the interests of agriculture. These districts could not suffer by the withdrawal of millions of people from the land ; on the contrary, such an emigration would better ensure their normal development. But at the time in question, when agriculture was declining, it would have been right to attend first of all to its reconstruction. This was the view taken by the non-party experts, and it had the support of certain communist leaders. But any such policy would have run counter to the feeling which had now come to dominate the communist party. The central point of the Five Year Plan was the extension of nationalised large-scale industry. This was to proceed at a rapid pace in all areas, in even the most remote and backward districts, so that everywhere a class of working men might come into existence which would serve to support the government of the proletarian dictatorship. The Five Year Plan was also regarded as a weapon in the war against the capitalist world. "The starting-point of the Five Year Plan for the development of the productive forces of the U.S.S.R.", we read,[1] "is the great task of overtaking and surpassing in the next historical period the level of the advanced capitalist countries and so to ensure the victory of the socialist economic system in its historic contest with capitalism. . . ." This contest was not thought of as being pursued by peaceful methods. For that reason the principal aim of the plan was not the development of agriculture, nor even the development of light industry, whose products might have been of immediate service to agriculture ; its aim was to develop heavy industry. Of the investments to be made into industry, 78 per cent are shared by the construction trades. By expanding the iron and chemical industries the armament of Soviet Russia is to be made secure. Great emphasis is laid on the development of the machine industry ; in order to make the Soviet Union absolutely independent of the capitalist world, even the most complicated machinery is to be built in the country.

The expansion of industry is not to increase its existing dependence upon the most important Russian coalfield, the Donetz basin. The greatest emphasis is laid upon the development of water power and on the exploitation of new coalfields, of coal seams of lower quality and of

[1] *The Five Year Plan* . . ., vol. i, p. 13.

peat deposits. The foundations were to be laid for an entirely new iron industry, on a very large scale, in a situation which was protected from the military point of view; this was to be accomplished by bringing the magnificent ore deposits of the South Urals (Magnitogorsk) into connection with the enormous coal-field of Western Siberia (Kuzneck). These districts were 2,400 kilometres apart.

The authors of the Five Year Plan were quite clear as to the dangers of a much too one-sided development. They did not wish to neglect the other branches of industry. The production of the construction trades (Group A) as planned by the Supreme Economic Council, was to increase in five years by 211 per cent while the production of the light industry (Group B) was to increase by 132 per cent. At the same time it was hoped to obtain an increase in agricultural production of 55 per cent. In the state farms (Sovchoze) and the peasant collectives (Kolchoze) a new socialist agriculture was to be developed. The peasants were to be collectivised voluntarily so far as it was possible to supply them with tractors and other machines; at the close of the Five Year Plan 13·6 per cent of the peasant holdings were to be collectivised. In the last year of the Five Year Plan it was expected that 25 per cent of all marketable agricultural products and 42 per cent of the marketable grain would be obtained from the socialist farms. The dependence of the market on peasant agriculture was thus to be greatly reduced.

The central question was how the enormous amount of capital necessary for all this economic development was to be procured. According to the calculations of the Gosplan, the capital of the Russian economic system—i.e.

original capital together with working capital—amounted in 1927–8 (in 1926–7 prices) to 84·8 mlrd. roubles, while in the year 1932–3 it was to amount to 161·4 mlrd. roubles (in fixed prices); thus the new investments of original and working capital (in to 1926–7 prices) are to amount to 76·4 mlrd. roubles, which is equal to 90 per cent of the old capital. The Five Year Plan bases no great hopes on foreign credits. Therefore this enormous sum must be saved out of current income. It is here, in the opinion of the Gosplan, that the miracle of planning will appear. By skilfully "fertilising" the labour of the people with capital and by transplanting the very latest technical achievements of western countries, and especially of America, on to Russian soil—by this means the national income (in fixed prices) is to be doubled in five years (more exactly, it is to be increased by 104·1 per cent).[1] In all departments of economic life, enormous progress will be made. Areas under cultivation are to be extended by 20 per cent, while production per unit of land is to increase in the following manner: wheat by a quarter, cotton by a third, flax by more than half, and so on. In five years the costs of production in industry are to be reduced by 35 per cent. The reduction in the building index of 41·3 per cent is considered to be of especial importance. Building costs are thus to be much less than if they were reckoned in stable prices. Thanks to the rapid increase in the national income, it will therefore be possible to invest 30·5 per cent of it without at the same time demanding any sacrifices from the people;[2] on the contrary, the portion of the income to be made available for the

[1] *The Five Year Plan* . . ., vol. i, p. 145.

[2] *Ibid.*, vol. ii, part 2, p. 38.

inhabitants of both town and country is to increase in five years by about two-thirds per head.

The co-operation of the non-party experts in the elaboration of the Five Year Plan is apparent in the fact that the plan is worked out on the basis not of a natural but of a money economy. Caution is to be exercised in regard to issues. On October 1st, 1928, the quantity of money was nearly 2 mlrd. roubles (1·97). In five years the issues were to amount to 1·25 mlrd. roubles, so that the quantity of money was only to increase by 63 per cent. In view of the important increase in the circulation of goods the value of money would actually have to rise; there was to be a reduction, over the five years, of the wholesale index by 17·6 per cent and of the cost of living index by 22 per cent.

The problem of market equilibrium is not forgotten. The "commodity famine" was to be finally overcome in two years. Thanks to the large increase in agricultural production the peasant would be glad to put his goods on the market. In order to tempt him, the so-called "scissors" were to be closed considerably, the retail index for industrial goods being reduced by 22·9 per cent and the purchase price index for agricultural products by only 5·4 per cent. In order to ensure obtaining supplies of agricultural products, these are stipulated beforehand (contracted for); that is to say, the peasant in his work of cultivation was to receive certain benefits from the government, while he in return agreed to deliver a definite quantity of his products at fixed prices in the autumn. The private dealer was not to be entirely eliminated from retail trading, but his activities were to be very much restricted; in 1927–8 his turnover still amounted to 25 per cent of the total retail figure, but in 1932–3 the percentage was to be 8·9 only.

All in all, the authors of the Five Year Plan were convinced that it would be possible in one way or another to maintain the equilibrium of supply and demand on the markets. "In our projects," they write,[1] "there are sufficient reserves, and in the plan system sufficient 'give', to enable us to make any unavoidable corrections of the parts without at the same time altering the whole; thus we shall finally secure the market equilibrium which we need."

As the whole plan is constructed from the point of a money economy, great attention is paid to the problem of financing it. The most important question is that of financing the investments. These amount altogether (in the current year's prices) to 74·2 mlrd. roubles.[2] Of this amount, 51·1 mlrd. roubles is supplied from the socialised sector.[3] Thus 23·1 mlrd. roubles, or 31 per cent of the total, must be provided by the private sector—of which peasant agriculture constitutes by far the greatest part. As to how this last and difficult task is to be accomplished, the authors of the plan do not greatly concern themselves. Of the 51·1 mlrd. roubles invested in the socialised sector, 31·50 mlrd., or 62 per cent, are to come from the profits (23·3 mlrd. roubles), and depreciation funds (8·2 mlrd. roubles) of the state undertakings themselves (in passing it may be noted that a considerable portion of the profits accrue to the treasury and are then redistributed by it). Thus the success of the Five Year Plan is first of all dependent upon whether the state undertakings, by operating efficiently and

[1] *The Five Year Plan* . . ., vol. ii, pt. II, p. 47.
[2] *Ibid.*, vol. i, p. 127.
[3] *Ibid.*, vol. ii, pt. II, p. 52.

economically, can really yield these great profits. Especially is this true of industry, into which (excluding house-building and electrification) 16·1 mlrd. roubles are to be invested, 15·7 mlrd. roubles of this amount being derived from profits and depreciation. Of the utmost importance to the financing of industry was to be a 35 per cent fall in the cost of its products. Of this 35 per cent, only 24 per cent was to be used for lowering prices, while 11 per cent was to accrue to industry as additional profit. This additional profit, derived from the lowering of costs, was to amount to 7·8 mlrd. roubles, that is to say nearly two-thirds of the total profits of industry.

The principal organ through which the finance plan is to be carried out is the budget. The treasury claims a far greater share of the national income than in a bourgeois state, just because the treasury assumes most of the responsibility for financing the national economy. Year by year, moreover, the state is to take an ever greater share of the national income, increasing from 24·4 per cent in 1927–8 to 31·1 per cent in 1932–3. According to the Five Year Plan, the revenue of the treasury—of the Union and the other political corporations—amounts to 51·0 mlrd. roubles;[1] of this 28·7 mlrd. roubles are derived from taxes, 13 mlrd. roubles from the share of the profits of state undertakings accruing to the treasury, 6·9 mlrd. roubles from internal loans, and so on. The characteristic feature of the socialist budget is the fact that 25·6 mlrd. roubles, that is about a half, was to be employed in financing the national economy.

But the socialist state cannot rest content with elabor-

[1] *The Five Year Plan* . . ., vol. ii, pt. II, p. 387.

ating its budget. If the general plan is to succeed, it is not sufficient that the budget shall be rightly handled; the entire life of the people must be subjugated to the plan. The full utilisation of the profits remaining in state undertakings, the activities of the co-operatives, the work of the credit system and of social insurance—all these must be supervised. A communist society presupposes such supervision, for no group interests or private interests may be permitted to come into conflict with the all-powerful state. Thus was the idea of a general finance plan arrived at. It embraces 86 mlrd. roubles, about half of the national income.

The Five Year Plan was conceived on the basis of a money economy, because even a socialist plan cannot be conceived in any other way. It is impossible to dispose over goods in kind.

III

ECONOMIC DEVELOPMENT AND ECONOMIC POLICY UNDER THE FIVE YEAR PLAN[1]

A. THE EVOLUTION OF THE SOVIET ECONOMY INTO COMPLETE SOCIALISM

THE Five Year Plan was at first not taken seriously abroad. It was regarded simply as agitation, as an attempt to make people work. This scepticism was carried too far; and when it was proved that in Soviet Russia much was actually being done to fulfil the de-

[1] In complete contrast to the N.E.P. period, when there was an abundance of Russian economic literature, any inquiry into Russia's economy during the Five Year Plan is much hampered by the shortage of basic material and its unreliability. The Institute of Economic Research was closed down when the Plan came into force; the Gosplan was thoroughly " purged " of non-party experts, and its monthly reviews were stopped in 1930. The last of the Gosplan's statistics, which appeared in book form, relate to the year 1929–30, and are definitely less valuable than previous issues. The Central Statistical Administration, which ranked as a separate department, was placed under the Gosplan in January, 1930, and " purged " of its best non-party experts. Statistics had now, by order, to " play a practical part in the war of communism against capitalism ". As a result of the dismissal of these impartial experts, most of the economic journals ceased to appear. The few that survived appeared only in connection with specific events and are filled chiefly by highly controversial articles aimed at Right and Left " deviations " or at " wreckers ". Even orthodox communists might not pronounce independent opinions without the risk of being accused in the same publication of deviating from the " general line ". Under the Five Year Plan only one single

mands of the plan, scepticism gave place to astonishment and even, in certain circles, to enchantment. But complete scepticism, no less than immoderate enthusiasm, was unjustified. Only in one respect was the attitude of the sceptics well founded: it was at once clear that the enormous capital expenditure referred to above was

book of statistics was published, and this dealt with the whole system. It contained not a word on the subject of prices, wages, or currency amongst other things. The survey published by the State Plan Commission in 1933, entitled *Results of the Completion of the Five Year Plan of Economic Development in the U.S.S.R.*, is silent as regards the most important facts and bears the stamp of a vulgar agitator's pamphlet (see my review: "The Completion of the Five Year Plan as officially described," in *Der deutsche Volkswirt*, of Jan. 12, 1934). One has the impression that the Soviet Government wishes to prevent any expert examination of its inflammatory literature.

Students of the Soviet economy have to fall back mainly upon the communist leaders' reports of the innumerable meetings held annually at New Year. The best sources of information are however the newspapers, for there one may still find, among the confused heap of inflammatory material, valuable news-items and surveys. Material taken from these sources must, of course, be used with discretion.

The laborious task of collecting scattered material from such sources and subjecting it to careful comparison and examination is carried out with great exactitude and patience by Professor S. N. Prokopovic's Economic Bureau in Prague. The monthly bulletins issued by this Bureau (in Russian) are most helpful to every student of the Russian economy. A more ambitious effort to edit the available material systematically was made by the Bureau of Research on Russian Economic Conditions at Birmingham University. Unfortunately only eight volumes of their Memoranda appeared (May 1931 to December 1932). A very valuable collection and competent survey of a large quantity of material is contained in an essay entitled *Die Bilanz des ersten Fünfjahrplanes der Sowietwirtschaft*, by Professor Dr. Otto Auhagen, a former German expert in Moscow. (Osteuropa-Institut in Breslau, *Quellen u. Studien, Abteilung Wirtschaft*. New Series, pt. 12, p. 75.) But research on economic development under the Five Year Plan is only possible on its general outline, for there are at present too many gaps in the material we need for information.

incompatible with a simultaneous improvement in the general standard of living. At the same time, it should not be forgotten that the communist state, with all resources at its free disposal and resting upon an absolute dictatorship, is the most powerful in the world ; while the subjects of such a state, unable to call anything their own, are the most impotent of all peoples. When it was necessarily shown that both goals could not be achieved at the same time, it was possible for the communist state not only to forgo any improvement in the standard of living, but even to depress it ; and this to an extent which would have been beyond the power of any bourgeois government. For in a bourgeois state the economic system is subject to laws of its own, which the government must respect ; and moreover even an autocratic bourgeois government is compelled to take some account of the feelings of the people.

The foundation of the Five Year Plan was the fact that enormous investments and enormous progress were to be made not only by nationalised, but also by private enterprise. The rapid development of peasant agriculture was to be of vital significance. But the truth is that even in the most favourable circumstances it is impossible to bring about any sudden development in this sphere. Agriculture, especially peasant agriculture, can only make comparatively slow progress, and then only in the most favourable conditions. The idea of making progress where the peasants, having achieved a minimum of prosperity, are persecuted, is out of the question. In 1928, for the first time since 1922, there was once more a shrinkage in the grain areas under cultivation ; 2·2 million ha. less were cultivated (97·1 mill. ha. in 1927 against 94·9 mill. ha. in 1928), while actually 4·3 mill.

ha. less were harvested (96·4 mill. ha. in 1927 against 92·1 mill. ha. in 1928).[1] The rate of increase in the amount of live stock was also very much slower. The government became aware of the consequences of this agricultural decline in the first year of the Five Year Plan. In 1928 no export of grain was achieved and the proposal of the Five Year Plan to found a very rapid economic expansion on the basis of a peasant agriculture was openly compromised.

But even in the sphere of socialised enterprise the Five Year Plan at once met with great difficulties. As a condition for its fulfilment it assumed the highest quality of labour. The plans of factory construction were to be punctually and accurately executed, and the process of rationalisation was to be so skilfully carried out that the work in progress in the factories was not to be interrupted for a moment. Colossal equipment was to be installed and put into operation without delay. All the most recent technical achievements were to be exploited in Soviet Russia. Only given such conditions could the great economies be made which were to make the correspondingly great investments possible.

But were these hopes as to the high quality of Soviet labour justified? Before the Five Year Plan came into force the Soviet system had already been in existence eleven years, and in this time it had not been able to show proof that its organisation was any better than that of Russian capitalism. Even before the Five Year Plan, when the construction of new factories was still on quite a modest scale, it was not possible to say that this constructional work had proceeded satisfactorily. It was slow and costly and its results were often far from

[1] According to "Control-Figures" for the Year 1929–30, p. 528.

satisfactory.[1] Soviet Russia did not possess a sufficient nucleus of experts and skilled workers to make possible the building operations called for by the Five Year Plan, and this lack could only be partly made good by help from abroad. The result was that the work was to a considerable extent carried out without any finalised plans. On the 1st April, 1930, only half (51 per cent) of the constructional projects possessed approved plans; a sixth (17 per cent) of them had rough plans and a third (32 per cent) no plans at all.[2] "We expend enormous sums," said Ordžonikidze, then head of the Commissariat of Worker and Peasant Inspection (R.K.I.)—the highest control authority of the union—on the occasion of a conference of industrial managers held at the beginning of 1931,[3] "but we do not know exactly the extent of the work which has really been done. . . . As a rule there are no estimates. We build thoughtlessly (Russian: čochom). . . . The result is that the cost of building is increased and there is a superfluity of workers, and so on." This sort of building was alone sufficient to create a serious breach in the finance plan.

But it was not only in building that no qualitative progress was to be expected; in the existing conditions the same was true of production. Before the Five Year Plan came into force no advantages in the socialist method of production were to be noted. The control figures for 1928–9 (p. 26) sadly observe "the efficiency of

[1] See my article, "Russian Industry and the Specialists" (*Der deutsche Volkswirt*, June 29, 1928, p. 1338–9).

[2] A. Mendelson, "The *Konjunktur* in the Economic System of the U.S.S.R. during the first half-year 1929–30" (*Planovoe Chozyaystvo*, 1930, No. 5, p. 217).

[3] *Izvestia*, of February 1, 1931.

fuels, raw materials and plant, remains much lower than before the war for almost the whole of industry (with isolated exceptions)." Accordingly in 1927–8, when the effect of inflation was still only slightly perceptible, the prime cost index was 185 (1913 = 100).[1] At the same time the quality of the products of socialist industry was lower than that of the former capitalist production.

Now according to the Five Year Plan, a very rapid increase of production was to be achieved not only by setting up new factories and extending the old ones, but also by means of a much more intensive operation of the latter. By introducing two and three shift labour, and by abolishing a general day of rest, it was sought to run the factories so far as possible without interruption. At the same time the greatest hopes were based upon the application of the very latest developments of modern technics. This absolute dependence upon technics, however, proved to be a mistake. The proper operation of new and complex machinery has proved much more difficult than its installation. In the new factories the so-called "growing-pains" of production lasted for years. Complicated machines are worn out and broken with extraordinary rapidity. New factories with the most up-to-date equipment often produce worse goods than the old, while their production costs are frequently higher. A new technique cannot be transplanted mechanically to foreign soil. It was precisely here that a selection should have been made, a selection which would take into account the special Russian conditions. Moreover, the exaggerated tempo at which everything was to take place created great difficulties. The factories

[1] *The Five Year Plan . . .*, vol. ii, pt. I, p. 433.

were filled with quite raw labour which was least qualified to deal with the intricate machinery.

The managers of industry, faced with the double task of producing rapidly increasing quantities of goods at ever lower costs, sought primarily to deal with the first part of their problem ; for it is easier to control the quantity of goods produced. According to the Soviet statistics, industrial production in the first year of the Five Year Period actually expanded at a somewhat greater rate than was foreseen in the plan. Production costs, however, were not so satisfactory ; in spite of every trick of accountancy, no amount of calculation could discover the looked for reduction.

Moreover, the calculation of costs was based upon the fiction that the quality of the goods had remained the same. In reality, however, the quantitative success was achieved by means of a standardisation of goods which, though very convenient for the producers, in no sense suited the requirements of the consumers ; and also by means of a systematic lowering of quality which degenerated into the mass production of inferior commodities. The quantitative increase in the aggregate of goods produced in no way represented an increase in its useful value.[1]

Thus at the outset the Soviet Government was confronted with the fact that the buildings cost more than the plan allowed for, and that socialist production was quite unable to provide the necessary funds for investments. In such circumstances it was possible to take

[1] See further my essay : " Der Fünfjahresplan und seine Erfüllung." *Weltwirtschaftliche Vorträge und Abhandlungen.* Edited by Dr. Ernst Schultze, Deutsche Wissenschaftliche Buchhandlung, Leipzig, 1932. Pp. 32–5.

one of two ways: either to curtail investments or to cut down the consumption of the people. The Soviet Government was not equally interested in all investments. Indeed, it renounced much of the investment which was proposed by the Five Year Plan for light industry, transport and so on. But in respect to that which constituted the essence of the Five Year Plan—the development of power stations and of the iron and engineering industry—the government made no sacrifices; on the contrary, it was decided at the sixteenth party congress of June-July 1930 to extend the plans in this direction. This decision was made partly in view of military considerations; and also with a view to achieving a very rapid mechanisation of agriculture—a new problem on the party agenda at this time. According to the Five Year Plan, the production of pig iron was to increase from 3·33 mill. tons in 1927–8 to 10 mill. tons, with a corresponding increase in the production of natural steel and rolled iron. It already appeared that such an increase could not be achieved. Nevertheless, the party congress decided to increase pig-iron production to 17 mill. tons. Moreover, the greatest emphasis was laid upon the expansion, on a scale two or three times greater than that proposed by the Five Year Plan, of the Magnitogorsk-Kuzneck iron combine; and it was precisely the development of this iron industry in the East that was most difficult and costly. It may be that these grandiose plans cannot be fulfilled, but they should certainly not be regarded as harmless dreams; for, generally speaking, the arrangements which the Soviet Government is making are in accordance with them.

Thus the investment plans were modified; but they remained very strained, and became still more so as a result of the decision taken by the same party congress that the Five Year Plan was to be completed not in five but in four years. Later the time for the execution of the plan was prolonged by three months, when a supplementary quarter-year from October-December 1930 was interpolated and the beginning of the economic year was postponed until January 1st. The abridged Five Year period was to end on January 1st, 1933, and not on October 1st as originally intended. In such circumstances the funds required for making the great investments could only be obtained by curtailing the consumption of the people. Naturally no such decision was ever formulated, but the whole economic policy of the Soviet Government necessarily tended in this direction.[1]

The financing of the investments had now to proceed on quite a different basis from that foreseen in the plan. A way out might be sought in an increase of the selling prices of industrial products. Yet this course was only partly open to a socialist planned economy. There was no particular sense in the raising of the prices of the means of production, for in the long run the selfsame state industry would have to pay for them. Only to a certain extent was there any point in keeping up the prices of consumption goods. According to the Five Year Plan, the prices of industrial products were to be reduced by 23 per cent. This, however, was quite out

[1] " Our country," we read in the *Five Year Plan* (vol. i, p. 70), " is making an unparalleled effort to expand its original capital at the cost of current economies, at the cost of a severe régime of thrift and of self-denial in respect of satisfying present needs in the name of the great historical tasks before us." Thus we see that the idea of enforcing fulfilment by curtailing the consumption of the masses was, despite all their protestations, not unfamiliar to the authors of the Five Year Plan.

of the question; on the contrary, the prices of consumers' goods were raised considerably on several occasions. In order to conceal the reduction of real wages, the publication of prices and indices were discontinued.[1] The consumers felt this increase of prices all the more since the goods were more and more standardised and less valuable.

In spite of the raising of the fixed prices of consumption goods and in spite of the fact that an increasing proportion of goods were sold in the so-called "commercial shops", the profits of light industry were unable to make good the losses on heavy industry. The magnitude of these losses may be seen from the following figures, which were published by accident. In 1932 the selling prices of rails for mines and for railways were 104 and 112 roubles per ton respectively, while their prime costs were 187 and 192 roubles per ton respectively. The subsidy required by the iron industry, which had become a charge on the state, amounted in 1932 to 450 mill. roubles.[2] According to the Five Year Plan, industry was to yield a net profit of 12 mlrd. roubles in five years; actually, in the shortened period, it yielded 5·6 mlrd. roubles, i.e. scarcely a half.[3] The same state of affairs was to be seen in all branches of the socialised economic system; in no case were the quality of labour or the profits which had been contemplated by the plan achieved. Thus the gaps which had appeared in the finance plan

[1] In the above-mentioned work issued by the Gosplan, *Results of the first Five Year Plan* . . . (p. 178), the allusions are exclusively to money wages—as if the Gosplan were quite unfamiliar with the notion of real wages!

[2] *Za industrializaciu*, of March 17, 1933.

[3] A. Putilov, "On the Problem of Industrial Economies and Savings" (*Planovoe Chozyaystvo*, 1932, pt. 5, p. 116).

owing to the inadequate quality of labour could only be partially filled by the increase in the price of consumption goods.

The other means available to the Soviet Government for financing the economic system was inflation; and it did indeed make use of inflation, though only to a comparatively modest extent. According to the plan, the quantity of money was to increase in five years from about 2 mlrd. roubles to 3·25 mlrd. roubles, the issues amounting to 1·25 mlrd. roubles. Information as to money issues are no longer issued; the last return of the Five Year period gives the quantity of money on July 1st, 1932, as 6·2 mlrd. roubles. But since the end of 1932 the issues have been very much increased, so that at the close of the Five Year period the quantity of money was 7 mlrd. roubles.[1] Instead of 1·25 mlrd. roubles, the issues made a total of 5 mlrd. roubles. They were four times as great as they should have been, and accordingly the quantity of money at the end of the Five Year period was more than twice as great as it should have been. The issues were sufficiently extensive to create a certain amount of confusion in the money economy, but they were not sufficient to make good the loss in net profit.

The reason why the printing presses were not able to offer adequate assistance to the government is to be found in the Soviet system itself; the fact is fundamental. In this system two sectors of society oppose one another, the socialist and the private; the first is primarily industrial and the second primarily agricultural (collectivisation has not altered the private character of agriculture, for it was not nationalised). The principal

[1] Cf. Auhagen, *Die Bilanz des ersten Fünfjahrplanes* . . ., p. 30.

aim of the Soviet Government is the rapid development of the nationalised heavy industry. In so far as this cannot be accomplished by raising the productivity of such industry, the private sector of society must be sacrificed. But least of all when economic conditions are left to develop spontaneously the inflation losses are borne by the farmers; for it is precisely they who have the disposal of products which are indispensable. Thus the inflation losses had to be borne by industry, and above all by the employees of industries ; yet the interests of the latter were nearer to the heart of the Soviet Government than were those of the peasant. It is therefore clear that the Soviet Government could not permit the inflation to operate freely and fully. It had to interfere, in order to shift its losses on to the peasants.

The only method by which this end could be gained was the forcible seizure of agricultural products at low fixed prices. Even before the Five Year Plan the inflation in its earliest stages had resulted in a return to the forcible expropriation of agricultural products. When the Five Year Plan came into operation this expropriation was carried out more and more thoroughly. The levies grow larger ; moreover, a principle was propounded to the effect that when a peasant, having delivered goods according to his assessment, is left with a surplus, he may not sell this surplus to private dealers (speculators) but must deliver it up to the state organisations. If the peasant could have exchanged the money he received for industrial goods at fixed prices his position would have been tolerable ; but industrial goods were brought into the country in ever smaller quantities. Thus, as had already happened under " War-communism ", the increasingly high assessments came near to being a downright expropriation of the peasantry. The home-workers found themselves in an analogous situation. They were collected into co-operatives and put under the supervision of co-operative Governing Boards, to whom they were forced to sell their products at fixed low prices. The home industries, which competed with large-scale industry for raw materials, were simply liquidated: and this was particularly injurious to the peasantry.

By forcibly expropriating the products of the private sector of society, and above all of agriculture, the prices of these products could be kept within certain bounds, and the principles of the plan, with their fixed prices, could be maintained. But with the progressive issues the discrepancy between the quantity of money and the fixed prices necessarily came more and more into evidence. The large-scale state undertakings could settle their accounts among themselves to a large extent by setting off the amounts in question, and the effect of the issues fell especially heavily on the consumption goods market. Thus the "commodity famine", so characteristic of the socialist system, became far more acute.

And goods also became scarce in the absolute sense. The government had destroyed the market in agricultural products and had taken upon itself the feeding of the masses; this task was much too difficult and could not be accomplished even by means of increasingly heavy levies. These levies gave rise to problems which the trading organisations were technically unable to overcome. Enormous quantities of the agricultural produce obtained—and even of produce which, like grain, was in its nature durable—were allowed to spoil, because no one knew how to deal with it.[1] And the manufactured consumption goods were also scarce absolutely. The consequence of industrialisation was an extraordinarily rapid growth of the non-agricultural section of the population. It increased from 32·4 mill. in 1928 to 47·4 mill. in 1932, i.e. by 15 mill. or 46·3 per cent. The demand of the industrial population for manufactured goods is many times as great as that of the agricultural population.[2] At the same time light industry had only expanded in so far as it had taken the place of the small-scale industry which had been abolished. When, in addition, we take into account the poor quality of the manufactured goods and the complete suspension of any import of consumption goods, it is clear that not only agricultural but also industrial goods must have become absolutely scarce under the Five Year Plan; scarce, i.e. even when measured by the modest standards of the unpampered Russian. Yet it would be a mistake to regard this shortage of commodities as the actual cause of the "commodity famine". Production may lag behind the needs of the mass of the people even in a bourgeois society, but this will never amount to a "commodity famine", even under inflation conditions; for a bourgeois economy always manages to maintain the balance between demand and supply. In such a

[1] Out of the enormous grain levy on the harvest of the year 1930, which amounted to 22·2 mill. tons, 25 per cent—that is, about 5·5 mill. tons—could not be got to the railway stations. This proportion of the grain either went bad or was stolen and never reached its destination (*Sovetskaya torgovlya*, 1931, No. 5, p. 12).

[2] In the year 1927–8, the consumption of industrial products was estimated at 35 roubles per head of the rural population and at 128 roubles per head (four times the amount) of industrial workers. (*Five Year Plan* . . ., vol. i, p. 101.)

system the mass of the people can never have the feeling that goods are scarce, but merely the feeling that money is scarce in their own case. It is different under a socialist plan, where the economic unsoundness of state undertakings usually leads to inflation. And as prices remain as nearly as possible stationary, a discrepancy arises between the quantity of money and the quantity of goods. What the consumer lacks is, not money, but the goods to spend money on. In a socialist economic plan, therefore, insufficient production is felt as a "commodity famine" rather than as a shortage of money.[1]

In such circumstances as these, goods could no longer be sold; it remained to distribute them. As early as spring 1929, six months after the Five Year Plan came into force, bread cards were introduced once more, and up to the autumn of the same year rationing was extended to all food-stuffs and all manufactured goods. The consistently planned-economy revealed itself as a consistent economy of force; everything was taken from the people, everything was distributed from above.

This was true not only of consumption but also of production goods. Production goods could no longer be

[1] For every phenomenon the communists have an explanation which glorifies their system. The "commodity famine" is explained in this wise for the benefit of the foreigner: Under Tsarism the peasants had had no use for manufactured goods, whereas their newly acquired prosperity and improved social standing now led them to demand them in enormous quantities, and industry was, in spite of its great development, unable at present to supply these. The post-Revolution mujik had become positively insatiable! Such trains of thought are often met with in travellers' reports, even in those which claim to have a scientific value.

traded, but had to be distributed ; the result was a new economic organisation of industry. Under the N.E.P. system all factories were collected into numerous trusts, according to their line of business and geographical situation. The trusts were closely connected with one another, so that a certain market developed even for the means of production. But even before the Five Year Plan came into force, as planning had become more important, so the interconnection of the market had ceased to play a part, and syndicates were set up over the trusts. The latter became responsible for supplying the means of production to numerous trusts in particular branches of industry and also for disposing of the products of these trusts. Under the Five Year Plan this centralisation of economic functions went on parallel with the destruction of the market, and it was finally confirmed by a resolution of the central committee of the party on the 5th December, 1929. According to this resolution all industrial undertakings were to be gathered, by trades, into Industrial Combines (Promob'ed-inenija). The functions of these Industrial Combines were very broadly defined : the work included the planning of production, the direction of capital buildings, technical direction, buying and selling organisation, the direction of commercial and financial operations, labour questions and the training and disposition of " Kadres " (that is, technicians and skilled workers). In this way the trusts lost their importance in favour of the Industrial combines.[1] Here, under another name, was a virtual reconstruction of the system which had already been put into practice under " War-communism " : the system of

[1] See article, " Fifteen Years of Soviet Construction ", *op. cit.*, p. 376–7.

" glavkismus ", of the strictly centralised management of industry.[1]

This development towards a strictly centralised socialism also found expression in a new credit organisation. Before the Five Year Plan came into force the elimination of private trading and the advance of planned-economy had already led to a simplification and concentration of the credit system. But there was still in existence a capitalist institution—namely commercial credit—which conferred upon the Soviet economy a certain elasticity. The state enterprises had the right to draw bills and give credit among themselves. This might have, to a certain extent, cut across socialist plans, and therefore commercial credit had to be abolished. This was accomplished by means of the Credit Reform of 31st January, 1930, which came into force on April 1st of the same year. According to this law, the provision of short-term credits became a monopoly of the state bank, and the state enterprises were forbidden to draw bills or give credit among themselves. The state bank acted between the buyer and seller; the latter sent his invoices to the bank, which credited him with the corresponding amount, while the buyer's account was debited. The Industrial Combines were to submit their credit plans punctually to the state bank; in these plans the credit requirements of every single factory and subsidiary were to be accurately set forth. It was hoped by thus concentrating credit in the hands of the state bank to fashion an effective instrument for supervising the execution of the plans.

[1] The word " Glavk ", or " governing board ", so detested in the days of War-communism, has been deliberately replaced by the name " industrial combine ".

Thus in the spring of 1930, and after the tremendous advance made towards the socialisation of agriculture in the previous winter, it seemed that the evolution of the Soviet economic system towards full socialism was complete. The Soviet Government disposed over all commodities, whether they were produced by state or by private enterprise. The means of production were apportioned to the various undertakings in accordance with the plans, and consumption goods were apportioned to the consumers in rations ("Pajki"). Money, which was issued liberally, was not the decisive factor in the distribution of goods. In the allotment of production goods the decisive factor was the verdict of an authority with full power to decide on the matter—generally an Industrial Combine—while in order to obtain consumption goods money again was not of essential importance, but rather the membership of a class whose work was valued by the state. Private trade, hardly tolerated as illicit traffic, could but vegetate in the most modest proportions.

In the sphere of foreign trade the evolution to complete socialism had this effect: the domestic value of export goods ceased to have any significance in estimating the foreign exchange to be obtained for them. In general the organisation of Russian foreign trade makes it possible for goods which are extremely scarce at home to be exported. Soviet Russia's foreign trade is a thing apart: such and such a quantity of goods must be imported (these goods under the Five Year Plan are devoted exclusively to industrial construction) and the price of these goods in foreign currency must be covered by a corresponding export of goods. Whether in view of the state of the internal market the goods concerned ought to be exported is a question which is not considered; nor indeed can their prices, which are fixed, provide any answer to the question. For this reason foreign countries have charged Soviet Russia with dumping. But in the case in question it is really something different, and an even greater evil. The expression "Dumping" has its origin in an economic order in which production costs are comparable with the proceeds. Here, however, the production costs at home are not comparable with the proceeds obtained abroad, so that the term dumping is hardly applicable.

For the masses this return to the "force economy" of War-communism was a bitter disappointment. Explanations had to be found for the increasing inadequacy of rations and for the progressively more shocking housing conditions. A scapegoat was wanted, and was provided by the intellectuals. There set in a period of the most appalling persecution, in which the intellectuals suffered even more than in the civil war. It was said that the intellectuals had obstructed the execution of the plans, even that they had acted treacherously on the instructions of capitalist countries. Thus the Soviet Government hoped, in a measure, to make amends for the suffering of the masses.

This economic development was reflected in the control-figures of the Gosplan for 1929–30 which were now drawn up for the first time without the assistance of the non-party experts by young communists. These figures are on a much lower level, scientifically, than those of the preceding years. The authors assign no importance to the problem of market equilibrium. They stand for the forcible expropriation of agricultural products and for the distribution of the same in rations; moreover, they are of the opinion that this distribution should be carried out strictly on class principles. They believe that " the expression of the national income in value form (in price) begins to lose its universal significance ". Yet they feel compelled to give utterance to certain feelings of apprehension : " This gives rise to new problems for economic analysis in general and for the analysis of the conditions of distribution in particular—problems which are solved neither by the theory of soviet economics nor by our statistics ". The young authors have not lost their faith in the essential possibility of solving the problem of natural socialism. But these control-figures were the last. After the currency was destroyed it was not possible to elaborate either well- or ill-founded finance plans and these constituted the kernel of the earlier control-figures.[1]

In 1930 the following views were dominant in economic literature—a literature now wholly enfeebled owing to the exclusion of the non-party experts : the N.E.P. system had been overcome, the Soviet economic system had already reached the stage of complete socialism. Money issues could be made without concern, for money was now nothing but an accounting symbol which one would soon be able to dispense with. One must accustom oneself to disposing over goods in kind. If, however, the Soviet economy did need a measure of value, then not money but the labour day was appropriate to socialism.

The economic ideology of the period of War-communism lived again.

[1] The programme figures in the communist leaders' speeches at New Year are still described as " control-figures ". But in fact these programme figures have no foundation whatever.

B. The Second Agrarian Revolution

The evolution to complete socialism led, in the sphere of agriculture, to a mighty upheaval which had in no way been foreseen by the Five Year Plan. This was a second agrarian revolution ; it uprooted the foundations of rural life much more radically, even, than the agrarian revolution of 1917–18.

The idea of the Five Year Plan, that rapid economic development could be accomplished upon a foundation of peasant agriculture, had proved itself mistaken from the outset. After the bad harvest of 1929 the government undertook to seize 13·9 mill. tons of grain from the peasantry, and in doing so it deliberately set out to ruin the well-to-do peasant. In this, indeed, it was successful ; but from then onwards, nothing more was to be expected from peasant farming, and it only remained to construct a new agricultural system in its place. The decision to do so was announced by the red dictator Stalin in his well-known speech of December 27th, 1929, at the Conference of Marxian Agrarian Politicians, and quickly put into practice. The task was to destroy the peasant system and to gather the peasants and everything that still remained in their possession into " Collectives " (Russian : Kolchoze). The internal structure of these collectives was not yet fully clear to the communists themselves.

The ruin of the well-to-do peasants provided a form of social support for the Soviet Government in its new undertaking. Of perhaps a third of the Russian peasants it was true to say that they had land, but no stock with which to farm it. In order to cultivate their land, the poor peasants had to depend upon their well-to-do neighbours ; they hired implements to cultivate their plots, or had their neighbours do it for them, or even leased their land for a share in the profit or for money. The ruin of the Kulaks at the same time deprived these poor peasants of their economic support, so that they were prepared to enrol themselves in the collectives which were favoured by the government. The flight of the rural proletariat to the collectives began. Politically this fact was of importance to the government. But economically it meant little as the rural proletariat possessed no stock.

The most important task remained—that of bringing the middle-class peasants into the collectives. These however would never have given up their own farms voluntarily. Only by force could the government achieve its purpose, and Stalin ventured on this perilous course. On January 6th, 1930, the political bureau decided to collectivise the Steppe areas by spring, and the other areas at a more moderate rate. Twenty-five thousand reliable communists were sent into the country armed with unlimited powers. According to their secret instructions, the well-to-do peasants and all who opposed collectivisation were to be turned out of their farms into the snow ; they were to be transported to the marshy forests of North Russia and Siberia to do forced labour (forestry, road-making, canal-building, and so on). Anyone who offered resistance was to be shot at once, without reference to the central authorities. This whole process was called " Dekulakisation " (Raskulačivanie). After twelve years the Soviet Government was sufficiently well organised and the peasants sufficiently disorganised to make possible a deed unprecedented in the history of the world. By these measures the peasantry was to be driven into the collectives, and indeed, at the beginning of March 1930, a good half of the Russian peasants had undertaken to enter these organisations. Nevertheless, there was a certain amount of resistance, both passive and active. Passive resistance was expressed in the mass-slaughter of live stock, which the peasants were supposed to deliver up to the collectives ; active resistance took the form of incendiarism, the murder of communists and—especially in non-Russian areas—of open revolt. Such revolts were not always easily crushed, owing to discontent in the Red army.

In his article of March 2nd, 1930 (" Going Giddy with Success ") Stalin abruptly suspended the forcible collectivisation, and declared that the Soviet Government had never ordered it at all. Actually he had realised that the political situation had become overstrained and also that the task of collectivising a good half of the peasants at a single stroke was from an economic point of view impossible. On the 15th March the central committee of the party permitted the peasants to leave the collectives. The greater part of the hurriedly created collectives collapsed. But in the Steppe regions any desertion of the collectives was now hardly possible, for here the sowing begins at this time.

The Soviet Government's retreat was only a manœuvre, with the object of pacifying the peasants. In the autumn of 1930 compulsory collectivisation was renewed ; the resistance of the peasants had meanwhile been broken, so that by early in 1931, more than 60 per cent of all peasant farms were already collectivised. In all economically significant areas the work was done. The only districts which remained uncollectivised were those —especially in the North—where peasant agriculture was of a purely autarchic character. From a political point of view, the difficult task of creating a socialist agriculture was accomplished.

But the intrinsic difficulties of this enterprise proved to be greater. Economically, the successful socialisation of agriculture is difficult if only because the advantages of large-scale farms are in general very questionable, and especially so the sphere of stock-raising. Moreover, the sudden break in the peasants' way of life completely upset them psychologically. And further, at the time when these events took place the intentions of the party had to a certain extent undergone a change.

At first the aim of the party had been to convert the peasants as quickly as possible into agricultural workers. Hence everything, even to the last hen, was to be socialised. Enormous losses resulted from this policy; the socialisation of the last cow, in particular, aroused immense indignation among the peasant women, for they relied upon this beast for their children's milk. This anger often found expression in specific peasant women's revolts (bab'i bunty).

Maybe this resistance could also have been broken down; Stalin, however, himself realised that the proposal to convert the peasants into agricultural workers was not in the interest of the Soviet Government. The mood of the great masses of the peasantry disquieted him. The latter, in so far as they felt it impossible to offer any resistance, relapsed into a state of resignation, into an attitude of mind which may be expressed in some such way as this: "All right, comrades, if you don't think we know how to farm, take over the management of the farms yourselves, and also the feeding of our families. We shall be quite agreeable to doing our seven hours' work under your orders, and we want the same privileges as the town workers enjoy." To Stalin this mood seemed dangerous. The aim of the Soviet Government was above all to make sure of securing the great levies ; the idea of assuming the responsibility for feeding the heavily over-populated rural areas was by no means tempting. The abandonment of compulsory collectivisation as announced in Stalin's celebrated article of March 2nd, 1930 was nothing more than a tactical manœuvre. On the other hand, Stalin's repudiation of the Commune was of fundamental importance. The Commune, in which the whole of peasant agriculture was to be socialised, was regarded simply as a convenient transition stage in the conversion of the peasants into agricultural workers. The aim now was to be not the Commune, but the "artel", a form of organisation in which production but not the domestic economy was to be socialised. However, this domestic economy was considered as having a fairly wide range. It was to include the fruit and vegetable garden, the vineyard, poultry, all the smaller animals and also a cow. In this way, certain elements of the private farm were to remain with the collectivised peasants. By thus defining fairly broadly the limits of the domestic economy it was emphasised that the peasants were not workers but members of co-operatives. But co-operatives in a communist state are fundamentally different from those in a bourgeois state. In the former there can be no question of their free development. The managerial committees of the collectives are elected according to the instructions of the party, and they consist of the most part of communists. The managers of the collectives are much more officials of the communist state than representatives of the members' interests. Their most important duty, on which their whole future depends, is to ensure the punctual delivery of the levies.

Moreover, the inner life of the collectives is controlled, not only by a statute, but also by innumerable government decrees. These decrees may regulate everything, down to the shoeing of horses. Thus the management of the collectives is more in the hands of the government than of the members ; on the other hand, the economic responsibility is shifted on to the latter. Only in this matter of responsibility are the collectives similar to bourgeois co-operatives or different from state enterprises. Moreover, the members of the collectives are not equally privileged. The managerial committee relies upon the so-called " Active ", which consists of former proletarians and stands in opposition to the former middle-class peasants. The latter feel themselves to be members of a second order, and often describe collectivisation as a return to serfdom.

With regard to the internal organisation of the collectives, the most important question is that of the division of income. The peasants' inclination was towards the equal distribution of income according to needs ; this inclination had its origin in the equal distribution of land which took place during the revolution, and also in the extreme inadequacy of the income itself ; the latter consists mainly of goods in kind, and after the levies have been deducted is at best only sufficient to satisfy the most elementary needs. Such a division has, moreover, the great advantage of simplicity ; no book-keeping is required. On the other hand, the system has a most unfavourable effect on the intensity of the work. The Soviet Government seeks to base the division upon the hours worked, and the efficiency and the quality of the work done, hoping in this way to increase the intensity and quality of labour. It would also like to introduce into agriculture, as in industry, the piece-wage system. But we should remember that the piece-wage system has not been extensively practised in capitalist agriculture, and this in spite of the employer's interest in increasing the intensity of labour ; for, in agriculture, an increase in the amount of work done may easily have a detrimental effect upon the quality of the work. In the conditions ruling in the Russian collective, there is still another drawback to the system of reward according to services rendered ; it calls for a very well-organised system of book-keeping, which in the absence of education cannot possibly be provided for the more than 200,000 collectives. The confusion existing in the organisation of labour naturally has a very unfavourable effect upon the intensity of the labour.[1]

Along with the collectivisation of peasant agriculture, the government took upon itself another task ; it set out to improve the economic organisation of the small number of great estates left in its hands after the agrarian revolution in 1917–18, and so to make more profitable use of them ; it also undertook the formation of new state farms. Of especial interest was the attempt to develop the so-called State Grain Farms (Zernosovchoze). This was begun as early as 1928. The intention was to develop very large farms (from 30 to 50 thousand ha.) in the Eastern dry region, these farms being devoted entirely to grain production and particularly to wheat. They were to rear no live stock whatever and were to

[1] See further my article, " Problems of Collectivisation in Peasant Agriculture in Soviet Russia," in *Berichte über Landwirtschaft*, 1932, vol. xvi, pt. 2, pp. 216–43.

be, as the saying went, 100 per cent mechanised. The entire organisation was to be equipped as an industrial undertaking, and for this reason these farms were described as " grain factories ". The Soviet Government spared nothing in the development of these grain factories. The work proceeded much more rapidly than had been foreseen, and in addition the average size of the farms was still greater than had been planned. By 1931 the areas under seed in the Zernosovchoze was more than 4 mill. ha.

As it had been proved in 1930 that collectivisation had an unfavourable effect on cattle breeding, the Soviet Government undertook the creation of very large Stock Rearing Enterprises, for which millions of head of cattle were seized from the peasants.

In spite of these efforts to create an entirely nationalised agriculture, it was impossible to get rid of the fundamental fact that Russia is a peasant country. In 1932 the State grain enterprises amounted to only 10 per cent of all the areas under cultivation, while in the case of the stock-rearing farms the percentage is much smaller still. As a result of the second agrarian revolution the collectives appeared as the decisively significant part of Russian agriculture. Agriculture, therefore, was not nationalised, and the rural population was not converted into agricultural workers. Nevertheless, an important step had been taken in the direction of complete socialism. In the managerial committees of the collectives the government now possessed valuable instruments for the carrying out of its plans and for the collection of its levies. Agricultural products were now much more open to seizure by the government than was the case before collectivisation. On the other hand, by gathering the peasants together the government created certain dangers for itself, for in the collectives the peasants were now organised.

C. The Attempted Return to Capitalist Forms

Although the Soviets' development on the lines of natural Socialism had the approval of the orthodox young intellectuals, it nevertheless gave rise to some concern within the Soviet Government. The government had been accustomed, at the time of the N.E.P., to regard the maintenance of economic calculation in its undertakings as being one of the most important pillars of its economic policy. Economic calculation, it saw clearly, was of the utmost significance if these undertakings were to operate efficiently. Since April 1st, 1930, when the Credit Reform came into force, the phenomena of inflation had been very much more in evidence. It was apparent to the government that lax credit conditions were undermining any proper system of economic calculation. When it was decided, at the end of the economic year 1929–30, to insert an entire three months into the period of the plan, the Soviet Government attempted to refrain from increasing the quantity of money during this period. But this attempt could not be carried out consistently. The managers of industry were so used to having money freely at their disposal that when credits were restricted they were unable to pay the workers' wages.

At the beginning of 1931 there was a Union Conference of Industrial Managers in Moscow. The description of the economic situation given by experts at this conference made a thoroughly depressing impression. It was clear the Soviet economic system was on the brink of general disintegration.

The gravest fact was the disappearance of economic calculation. Under the N.E.P. when the means of production could be obtained on the market every enterprise reckoned with money, tried to be thrifty and to make profits. Now the acquisition of the means of production depended not so much on money as on the decisions of the Governing Boards. Once the plans were sanctioned by the government, money for their execution could always be obtained from the state bank. "With us," said Ordžonikidze, president of the Workers' and Peasants' Inspection (R.K.I.), at the conference referred to, "with us the state bank pays for everything, and the undertaking is materially responsible for nothing at all. . . . Wages are paid without reference to you (the industrial managers). Goods are paid for regardless of quality, people take your products away and distribute them." "That's grand," was the ironic comment of the audience. *Za industrializaciu*, the organ of the Supreme Economic Council, writing on the situation in its leading article of December 19th, 1930, said: "Among industrial managers there is a popular notion that however great the financial deficits, the State will always make them good; for finance is not to impose any limits on the expansion of production, and the extension of capital construction." Thus the managers of undertakings became accustomed to carrying out the plans without sparing either the means of production or labour.

The other great mistake was the unprofitable distribution of producers' goods. As there was a surplus of money in relation to these, all manufacturers tried to produce the largest possible supplies. They did not mind having them on their hands so long as they were sure of them when the demand came. It is a characteristic of the capitalist system that goods are stored by their respective producers and are available for consumers (by which is meant productive consumers) if and when they are able to pay for them. But under the conditions resulting from the socialist inflation, producers' goods found their way quickly to the consumers' storerooms, where they were not accessible to other consumers. In this way some factories would be in possession of immense stores of certain goods while others were left entirely without them. The Industrial Combines which controlled distribution were not in a position to carry out their task satisfactorily, for, given the conditions, prices could be no guide to them. The idea that these Governing Boards were capable of judging the quantity of producers' goods required by individual factories arose from a widespread but fallacious assumption of the omnipotence of socialist central bureaux. Such omniscience is obviously impossible, since producers' goods are complementary and the lack of one or other special product may well suffice to paralyse production, even though there be a surplus of the article in question in the country.

The Credit Reform, which came into force on April 1st, 1930, and in which people had hoped to see the culmination of the planned economy, also contributed much to the disorganisation of the economic system. The state bank was no more than a financial institution, and was quite incapable of controlling the execution of the plans, or, therefore, of deciding upon their credits. In order not to hinder the plans it shaped its credit policy on very liberal lines ; with the Credit Reform begins the period of "automatic" crediting, while at the same time all credits throughout the system became frozen. In the first one and a half years after the Five Year Plan came into force, from October 1st, 1928, to March 31st, 1930, the quantity of money increased by 875 mill. roubles, but in the following half-year the increase was 1,388 mill. And in yet another respect the Bank Reform had a demoralising effect on business management. Immediately the bank received the invoices for the goods consigned it debited the purchaser's account with the price of the goods; thus the purchaser lost all control over the way in which the order was executed. The newspaper, *Izvestia*, in its leading article of March 22nd, 1931, summed up the effects of this credit system as follows:

> This way of making credits led, by its very nature, to the complete liquidation of the contract principle between the undertakings and associations; and this inevitably had a weakening effect in the struggle for quality and variety in production, in the carrying out of the plan to make savings and earn profits, and in the attempt to reduce costs. The commercial and financial activities of the undertakings were left out of account. Questions of finance do not interest the heads of undertakings at all.

In addition, the exaggerated development of planning also had a very unfavourable effect on the distribution of consumers' goods. It would be a mistake to assume that the extraordinary decrease in the supply of consumption goods received by the population was due entirely to the failure of production, for to a very large extent it was due to faulty distribution. The victory of complete socialism brought with it not only the suppression of private trading, but also a fundamentally new and planned system of distribution. The wholesale stores in the provinces, which formerly supplied the local co-operatives, were gradually closed down ; but the local co-operatives were not then empowered to deal directly with the Industrial Combines. The latter made general contracts with the Centrosojuz (Consumers' Co-operative Central) and the Centrosojuz then distributed the goods throughout the immeasurable Russian territory according to plans drawn up *a priori* in Moscow. In order to avoid intermediate trading agencies, the factories sent the goods in small consignments to the most remote local co-operatives in accordance with instructions received from the Centrosojuz (the so-called transit-trade).

With this system of general contracts and transit-trade, therefore, planned economy in the sphere of consumption goods reached its fullest development. But the difficulties which always confront planning were particularly in evidence. This system might have functioned excellently if the Centrosojuz had been omniscient. Unfortunately it was not, and the result was that the distribution of consumption goods fell into a condition which, even in the opinion of the managers of the Centrosojuz, was chaotic.[1]

And yet serious gluts, such as so often occur under capitalism, could not occur under this system. In order to obtain his allotted piece of bread the consumer had to come to the co-operative store. This provided an opportunity of forcing him to buy other goods, even though they were quite unwanted and of the worst quality (the so-called " compulsory assortment "). In

[1] See pronouncement by the president of the Centrosojuz Zelenski at the 15th Soviet congress of the R.S.F.S.R. (*Izvestia*, of March 7, 1931) ; extracts in my *Five Year Plan* . . ., pp. 83–4.

conditions of "commodity famine", moreover, the consumer had no particular interest in saving his money. Thus, however great the confusion in distribution, however bad the quality of the goods, they were sold. The consumer was still the only sufferer.

The inner meaning of this whole development was a partial relapse of the economic plan, originally designed on a money basis, into a condition analogous to that of natural socialism; yet the unsoundness of this system had already been proved by experience.

The conditions described were discussed once more at a conference of industrial managers which took place in June 1931. The conference was held in secret; Stalin's programme speech, which was made to the conference on June 23rd, was only published on July 5th. This speech was of fundamental importance for the economic policy of the Soviet Government in the period which ensued. It did not suggest in the least that the government was renouncing the principles of planned economy and socialism, nor was the freeing of private trade envisaged. But the new tone in Stalin's speech reflected the conviction which, since the beginning of the third year of the Five Year Plan, had become general among all influential industrial managers, namely, that the maintenance of certain capitalist institutions was an absolutely essential condition for the fulfilment of the socialist plans. Complete socialism was in essence still conceived as natural, but people believed that the N.E.P. system had not yet been entirely eradicated, and that the money economy, the most important principle of the N.E.P., must be preserved. In his speech of June 23rd, 1931, Stalin strongly condemned the idea of a moneyless economy for the current period, describing it as a

" Trotskyite " movement to the left. Economic calculation was recognised as the main principle of the Soviet Economy. " Control by Rouble " (" Poverka rublem ") —such was the slogan.

To this end the Credit System had above all to be reconstructed. By means of a series of Credit Reforms it was sought in 1931 to compel the managers of industry to return to strict methods of economic calculation. Here again no renunciation of socialism is to be perceived. Bill credit was still forbidden, and the state bank was still the only body empowered to give short-term credits. But the Soviet Government realised that the state bank could only function as a financial institution. In order to avoid a further freezing of credits, all undertakings were instructed to show their balance sheets and to determine exactly their requirements of credit. Their own funds must be kept strictly separate from funds borrowed from the bank. Short-term credits could only be sanctioned for quite definite purposes, and must be repaid punctually under threat of economic reprisals.

Direct relations between buyers and sellers was to be renewed. On this account all state enterprises were to conclude forward contracts among themselves, these contracts to be sanctioned by the higher courts superintending the execution of the plans. Such contracts were to specify exactly the assortments and qualities as well as the prices and quantities of the goods to be delivered. The state bank was entitled to credit the supplier with the value of the goods consigned when the latter had been accepted by the purchaser. Thus the producer's activities were really controlled not by the bank, but by the customer.

In 1931 certain steps were taken to lessen the bureaucratic character of the Industrial Combines. It is true that the trusts were not restored to their former position of importance, but the Industrial Combines were divided up according to specialities or territories. A conviction was felt that undertakings of too great a size could not be controlled. The " giganto-mania " which had developed in the preceding years was condemned. An attempt was made to divide up excessively large undertakings into smaller ones. In so far as this was not possible, the separate departments of large undertakings were to carry out separate economic calculations.

The centralisation of all profits with the treasury was recognised as harmful. In accordance with the decision of the Council of People's Commissars, of May 3rd, 1931, about a half of the profits were to be left with the undertakings. These profits might be used for capital construction, for increasing their working capital, or to satisfy the cultural requirements of their employees.

In regard to the distribution of goods, Stalin coined the expression " Soviet Trade ", which was to take the place of " Socialist distribution ". Contact with the consumers was again to be sought. The wholesale stores in the provinces were to be re-established, and the dispatch of small consignments in accordance with instructions from above (transit-trade) was to be discontinued. Goods were not to be forced upon customers, and where possible they should not be distributed as rations. Only those goods should be rationed of which there was an obvious deficit.

Changes were to be made in the organisation of labour. A sense of responsibility was to be encouraged among individual workers, both in regard to the quantity and quality of their labour. The five-day week and the uninterrupted running of factories which went with it, was to be abolished ; this system had destroyed the workers' responsibility for the condition of machines and tools. In order to increase the intensity of labour, it was sought to make piece-wages general. In selecting managers it was recommended that not only their party membership, but also their qualifications for the work should be taken into account.

This attempt to maintain within the socialist framework certain capitalist institutions was not altogether without results, and it saved the Soviet economy from final collapse. Credits not being so freely available as before, many of the industrial managers were compelled to take some account of money, and so to introduce some sort of order into production. Here and there the accumulation of useless stocks of production goods was abandoned, and such stocks were realised in order to provide the undertakings with urgently necessary working capital.

Nevertheless, these successes remained very modest ; for the capitalist institutions belong to a fundamentally different economic system, and whether socialism can assimilate them remains questionable. Again and again the planned economy imposes upon the socialist enterprises tasks which must be antagonistic to profit-earning. Thus these new tendencies do not penetrate the system sufficiently deeply.

The state bank has no adequate means of forcing credit discipline upon the state enterprises. Technically it could now seize their goods, but actually it does not dare to take a course which runs counter to the execution of the plans. The trusts, when heavy pressure is brought to bear on them in regard to the reduction of costs, often suggest that certain definitely unremunerative concerns should be closed down ; but the authorities do not acquiesce, believing that such measures would be capitalistic rather than socialistic.

The most important question, so far as the managers of industry are concerned, is the superficial execution of the plans ; and, indeed, their future mainly depends upon this. It is precisely in the sphere of building activity—which plays so important a part—that no attention whatever is paid to profitability. It has been shown (*Izvestia*, Nov. 15th, 1931) that in many cases those in charge of construction works have no knowledge at all of the estimates, and that they do not even know by how much the estimates have been exceeded. Their point of view is generally something like this : " It is important to complete the work to time, and how much it costs is a detail ". They are of the opinion that rapid building is incompatible with low costs. Thus are finances managed in the most important sphere of the planned economy. But even in the sphere of industrial production where costs can be set against returns, the position is not essentially different. Here the most important question for the managers is still the quantitative fulfilment of the plan, and they are far less concerned about profitability or about the quality of the products. For this point of view remains in essence the point of view of the Soviet Government.[1]

It is, moreover, impossible to replace a " socialist distribution " of consumption goods by trade as long as

[1] In the report of the State Plan Commission : " The Results of the Completion of the first Five Year Plan . . .", the Government seeks to prove that the plan has reached completion ; yet questions of prices, costs, remunerativeness are not considered.

the great discrepancy continues to exist between the quantity of money and the fixed prices of the goods. If one really wishes to change over from socialist distribution to trade, then one must break with the system of fixed commodity prices.

In order to make any serious differentiation between real wages, the Soviet Government would have to have at its disposal greater quantities of foodstuffs and sufficient dwelling accommodation ; as long as it has not, any increase in the real wages of one worker must seriously prejudice another.

The government's desire that in the selection of managers practical qualifications as well as political opinions should be taken into account remained a pious hope. Socialism involves the most intimate association of politics and economics ; nor can it be otherwise.

In spite of the measures taken, money issues could not be sufficiently restricted. In the two years from January 1st, 1931, to the end of the Five Year period the quantity of money rose from 4·3 mlrd. roubles to about 7 mlrd., that is by 2·7 mlrd. roubles. But in so far as the government did not wish to permit itself still greater issues, it was compelled to restrict the building programme. In the *Ekonom. Žizn'* of September 12th, 1931 (and nowhere else ; there was apparently a desire not to give this decision wide publicity), there was published a decree of the Supreme Economic Council, to the effect that all building which could not be completed in that year was to be discontinued for the time being ; and that all building materials must be transferred to those buildings which could be finished that year. In this way large quantities of capital were immobilised in unfinished buildings.

D. The Symptoms of Crisis at the end of the Five Year Period

In spite of the preventive measures taken by the government, severe crises have occurred in the Soviet economic system since 1931. These are partly the result of the discrepancies which must inevitably arise where economic development has been forced to take place at an exaggerated pace. The rapid construction of the heavy industry—especially in the East, with its enormous distances—had subjected the Russian railways to a much heavier strain than had been foreseen in the Five Year Plan. As the principal means were wasted for the development of the heavy industry, the railways could not be adequately equipped. The available rolling-stock had to be used ever more intensively. The absence of economic calculation contributed not a little to the uneconomic running of the railways ; similar kinds of goods were carried long distances in opposite directions, and bulky consignments of small value were sent on enormous journeys. Although in 1931, 151·9 mlrd. ton-kilometres were carried, and the work done by the railways exceeded what was originally planned by nearly 25 per cent, the demands of the economic system were not met. This had a particularly unfavourable effect on the iron industry, which in this year actually suffered a serious set-back ; production of sheet iron fell from 4·99 mill. tons in 1930 to 4·06 mill. tons in 1931, a decrease of 18·6 per cent. In spite of very considerable imports of sheet iron, which amounted to 1·41 mill. tons in 1931, the lag in this industry, which was also accompanied by an insufficient production of coal, checked development in all departments of the economic system.

But the greatest difficulties arose in agriculture. Here the effect of socialisation on production was quite different from what the Soviet Government had anticipated.

There could be no two opinions as to the effect of collectivisation on live-stock farming; the effect was collapse, nor was there any recovery in this sphere. On the contrary, the falling off in the quantity of cattle continued even after complete collectivisation. The essential contradiction between cattle farming and socialism became patent, for it is precisely in cattle farming that an individualistic organisation is of decisive importance.

The effects of collectivisation in grain farming were at first not as unequivocal. It chanced that weather conditions in 1930 were excellent; thus the communist leaders were led to declare, at the 16th Party Congress of June–July 1930, that the grain problem, hitherto so acute, was "solved". And indeed from the harvest of 1930 22·2 mill. tons of grain were obtained, that is twice as much as in the years of the N.E.P. Of this harvest it was possible to export 6·2 mill. tons of grain, more than half of the average pre-war grain export (11 mill. tons); and since the social revolution so extensive a grain export had never yet been achieved.

But one question remained; were these great grain-levies, amounting almost to what was brought to the market before the war, the fruit of an improvement in grain farming, or were they simply an expression of the greater power of the Soviet Government in the rural areas? The Soviet Government believed the first explanation to be true. It asserted that grain farming, thanks to its mechanisation, had made enormous progress. This view was erroneous. The tractors which were collected in the so-called machine-tractor stations, could not possibly make good the tremendous decline in the number of draught horses. Any careful cultivation of the fields was out of the question. In fact all observers of Russian agriculture maintain that the land never looked so neglected and so rank with weeds as just after collectivisation. Regular manuring, such as is required by the fields in the North and even in the Northern black earth area, was impossible.

The great hopes which the Soviet Government based on the mechanisation of agriculture were the outcome of an identification of agriculture and industry. But agriculture is concerned with organic processes which cannot be decisively effected by the mechanisation of labour ; it is a different thing from industry which is not dealing with living material. Mechanisation as applied to agriculture can only be of service in a system of cultivation that ensures a rational and careful cultivation of the soil. In isolation it can give no positive results. Moreover, it proved much more difficult to transfer the methods of mechanised agriculture to Russian soil than the Soviet Government had imagined. The tractors did not work so efficiently in Russia as in America. It was difficult to repair them quickly or to provide them with spare parts. They wore out so rapidly that their profitability was doubtful.

The experience of the state grain farms showed especially clearly how ill-founded were the great hopes which the Soviet Government based on mechanised agriculture. In the dry eastern steppes are to be found the best conditions for the use of tractors and other agricultural machines, such as mowing threshers. People were convinced that excellent results would be obtained here ; abroad it was announced in advance that the Soviet

Government could produce grain in these socialist undertakings cheaper than was possible in capitalist farms. Thus the Soviet Government sought to explain to the world why it could sell its grain at any price it would fetch. Without the use of tractors the rapid development of the state grain farms would certainly have been impossible. But their harvests were considerably lower than the average for the country, and no higher than that of the peasant farms of the same area. There could be no question of any increased ability to resist drought. Owing to the rapid wearing out of tractors the profitability of the large-scale farms is very doubtful.[1] These farms have now been reformed in so far as they practise a less unbalanced rotation of crops and as grain farming is combined with stock raising; moreover, the farms have been divided into smaller undertakings.

The state grain farms proved how mistaken must be any attempt to treat agriculture in the same way as industry. And if the mechanisation in the state grain farms produced no outstanding successes, how much less was to be hoped from the collectives. The economic and social conditions in the collectives were extraordinarily complex and, moreover, the government was not in a position to supply them with a sufficient number of tractors.

Collectivisation, therefore, did not as yet mean technical progress. It was simply a revolution in the social

[1] See further my article, " Die ' Getreidefabriken ' als ein Versuch des Wiederaufbaus und der weiteren Erschliessung der Trockengebiete." Joint publication by B. Brutzkus, V. v. Poletika and A. von Ugrimoff. " Die Getreidewirtschaft in den Trockengebieten Russlands. Stand und Aussichten ", 67th Supplement of *Berichte über Landwirtschaft*, 1932, pp. 113–32. See also Prof. Dr. Zoerner's *Das Agrarexperiment Sowietrusslands* (Paul Parey, Berlin, 1932).

organisation of agriculture which enabled the Soviet Government to collect great levies more easily. But to collect great quantities of grain from an exhausted agriculture must eventually lead to catastrophe. The Soviet Government, assuming that socialist agriculture had nothing to fear from a bad harvest took no account of the drought of 1931 ; and when in that year it again commandeered an enormous grain-levy of 23 mill. tons—of which 4·5 mill. tons were exported—the Steppe regions and the whole of the Ukraine were plunged in a famine such as had not been experienced in Soviet Russia since 1921–2. These vast levies utterly disheartened the collectivised peasants, and they became much less willing to work. In spite of satisfactory weather in 1932, the harvest for this year was also poor. The Soviet Government was compelled to reduce the levy for the 1932 harvest by 20 per cent, but even so the demand was much too severe for an exhausted agriculture. And then the Soviet Government began to feel a certain disillusionment so far as the collectives were concerned. The collectivised peasants attempted to conceal the harvests ; the managing committees—often even those which consisted of communists—were inclined to protect the people from the exorbitant demands of the government. The levies had to be collected by punitive expeditions, as a result of which not a few of the communists in charge of the collectives were shot. The severe famine lasted even after the harvest of 1932.[1] All departments

[1] For the results of the collective experiments in the grain industry, see my article, " Russlands Getreideausfuhr, ihre wirtschaftlichen und sozialen Grundlagen und ihre Aussichten " (*Weltwirtschaftliches Archiv*, October 1933, pp. 489–99). There is an excellent description of the state of Russian agriculture at the end of the Five Year Plan in the report of the German agricultural expert in Moscow, Dr. Otto Schiller :

of economic life suffered in sympathy, so that the Five Year period came to an end in a state of acute crisis.

The Soviet Government was compelled to reduce exports of grain harvested in 1932. The result was a sharp decline in the imports required for industrialisation.

In industry, also, labour was seriously affected by the famine. As early as spring 1930, after the first effort at compulsory collectivisation, animal products had vanished from the towns. At the same time, owing to the rapid increase in the number of workers, dwelling accommodation had become much more unsatisfactory. The lack of food and accommodation was so acute that even the unspoilt Russian workers from the villages could not tolerate it for long. Again and again they returned to the villages, only to seek far and wide for fresh employment under better conditions. Thus there developed in the course of the Five Year period an enormous fluctuation of industrial workers. This made well-regulated labour hardly possible. As the food situation in the towns grew worse, so the efficiency of the workers decreased.

According to the Five Year Plan, it was anticipated that the increase of industrial production would be greatest in the last year; it was to rise by 25 per cent. This forecast was based upon the assumption that in the last year a particularly large percentage of the new factories would be put into operation. This, indeed, took place. According to the report of the Gosplan, factory and plant to the value of 15·3 mlrd. roubles were put into operation during the Five Year period, and of this total factories and plant to the value of 5·7 mlrd.

" Die Krise der sozialisierten Landwirtschaft in der Sowietunion." 79th supplement of the *Berichte über Landwirtschaft*, 1933.

roubles were put into operation in the year 1932.[1] Thus an enormous increase of production was expected. But owing to the reduced capacity of the workers and the failure of several key industries, the increase of industrial production almost came to a standstill. The gross value of the production of nationalised industry amounted to (in 1926–7 prices) 7·6 mlrd. roubles in the first quarter of 1932, 6·9 mlrd. in the second and 6·7 in the third.[2] Altogether the production of planned industry in 1932 showed an increase of 8½ per cent over the previous year. While the production of planned industry in 1932 was greater by 6·6 mlrd. roubles than the previous year, the increase in the following year was only 2·1 mlrd. roubles.[3] The great sacrifices made by the country in order that industry might be expanded seemed in the face of the growing economic confusion to have been in vain.

At the conferences which took place in January 1933, after the end of the shortened Five Year period, the communist leaders declared that the plan had been successfully carried out. Nevertheless, the second Five Year Plan, whose general outline had been made public as early as January 1932, and discussed in numerous conferences in the following months, had to be postponed. "I will not drive and whip the country any longer," Stalin declared in his speech of January 7th, 1933. There was surely no reason for this restraint if the Five Year Plan had really been carried out. According to the plan, the real income per head of population available for

[1] *Results of the Completion of the Five Year Plan* . . ., p. 47.

[2] Professor Prokopovič's Bulletin No. 100, of December 1, 1932; pp. 16–17.

[3] *Auhagen*, *op. cit.*, p. 66.

purposes of consumption was to increase by two-thirds. After the fulfilment of the Five Year Plan the people ought really to have felt thoroughly satisfied with the state of affairs, and ready and willing to enter upon a second Five Year Plan which promised them even greater riches. The postponement of the second Five Year Plan resulted simply from the fact that the first had not been carried out. The principal aims of the year 1933 were to be the completion of the capital buildings commenced in the previous year and the efficient operation of the new factories. It was realised that this latter task had proved to be much more difficult than the actual construction of the factories. Thus although the first Five Year period was considered closed at the beginning of 1933, it would in fact have been more correct to include 1933.

E. Economic Policy at the close of the Five Year Plan

In order to overcome the crisis phenomena which had appeared at the close of the Five Year period, the Soviet Government took two series of measures. These, to a certain extent, came in conflict with one another.

Above all the Soviet Government sought to discipline the discouraged masses, to force them to stick to their work. So far as industry was concerned, every means was to be employed to prevent that widespread movement of labour which was having so fatal an effect upon the workers' efficiency.

It is in the essence of a planned economy that the state cannot be satisfied with the power of disposing over the material means of production alone. It must also claim the right to control the most important non-material means of production—the human labour force. This characteristic of the planned economy had already appeared under "War-communism", and since labour had become scarce under the Five Year Plan, it had emerged again. In order to secure for itself power over the workers, the government discontinued, by its decision October 9th, 1930, all payment of unemployment benefit. The employment bureaux were empowered to allot work to the unemployed away from their domicile and irrespective of their qualifications. The employment bureaux also received the right to transfer persons already in employment to other situations without taking into account their present place of residence. It was sought to stop the frequent change of employment on the part of the workers. Yet in spite of all this the government was not at that time successful in subordinating the workers. Owing to the rapid development of building and industry qualified workers were in strong demand and welcome everywhere; for that reason it was difficult to enforce measures which restricted their free movement. As for the labourers, most of them had ties with the village. They disappeared into the villages in order to obtain other positions later. But it was impossible to found a planned economy on free labour alone. In order that important branches of industry might not be neglected, the government found itself compelled to create great armies of forced labourers. This forced labour, which was to supplement the services of the free workers, was drawn from the "dekulakised" peasants and various political suspects.[1] Thus the great develop-

[1] For a detailed description of forced labour in Soviet Russia, see Memorandum 1 of the Birmingham Bureau.

ment of the lumber industry in the bleak and little colonised regions of North Russia and Siberia was founded mainly upon the forced labour of convicts in concentration camps. This was supplemented by obligatory services performed by the local population. The last great achievement of the Soviet Government—the cutting of the White Sea Canal under the very difficult conditions ruling in the far North—was carried out entirely by convict labour. The entire labour management was handed over to the State Political Administration (G.P.U.) which organised the work by its own special methods. The convict army was of such a magnitude that the G.P.U. found it possible to have this great work performed with only the most primitive tools.

The tremendous movement of labour which was taking place at the end of the Five Year Plan compelled the government to make new efforts to prevent it. It now attempted to solve the problem by plan. A very strict passport system was introduced ; beginning with the large cities, the inhabitants of the small towns and all important districts were gradually compelled to obtain passports. In this way the Soviet Government at last secured control over the workers' activities, with the power to tie them to their jobs. Moreover, the passport system enabled the government to rid the large cities of inconvenient sections of the community, the feeding of which had been very troublesome.

At the same time stern measures were taken to discipline the workers. As early as 1930 careless work in certain particularly important posts (tractor and locomotive service and so on) had been dealt with as criminal. At the end of the Five Year period a new and quite savage step was taken (Government decree of 15th

November, 1932). Any wage-earner absenting himself from his employment for a single day without giving a good and recognised reason was to be discharged with the loss of his food- and room-cards ; at the same time he was forbidden to take other employment for six months.

The Soviet Government, having entrenched itself so deeply into the life of the rural population, and having destroyed its former economic organisation, was also faced with the difficult task of disciplining the country people. The great levies, which had left the agricultural population without food, led to attempts on the part of members of the collectives to provide for themselves independently out of the collectivised harvest. Before harvest-time they would creep out secretly at night on to their own fields ; they would cut off the ears of corn and stuff them into sacks so as to make sure of a little grain before the levies were collected (such malefactors were termed " hair-dressers "). These and similar phenomena became very widespread. According to the law of August 17th, 1932, such independent disposal of social property was punishable by death. From January 1933, departments of the G.P.U. were set up in all state farms and machine-tractor stations. For this purpose 15,000 communists were sent out from the towns. They were given unlimited powers in superintending the work of the collectivised and also of the private peasants. For careless work or for failure to carry out the plans they could impose the severest penalties, including death. In this way a sort of siege of agriculture was instituted ; such was the description applied to these measures by Dr. Otto Schiller, the German agricultural expert.[1]

[1] *Die Krise der sozialisierten Landwirtschaft* . . ., p. 78.

Alongside of these measures to organise labour upon a foundation of the most rigid discipline another tendency became evident in the Soviet Government's economic policy. In the spring of 1932 the agricultural population found itself in a condition of profound depression. The Soviet Government began to doubt whether it paid to confine the entire economic activity of the masses within the framework of the plan, for such a policy induced a mood of utter despair and had an unfavourable effect upon the willingness of the people to work. In 1932 the grain levies were reduced, and in the following year they were replaced by grain purchases at fixed prices, in quantities based upon the planned (and not real) areas under cultivation ; and by the purchase of animal products at low fixed prices in quantities based upon the stocks of cattle. The quantities were fixed high, and they were fixed higher in proportion as the degree of socialisation of the farms concerned was less. At the same time the local authorities were strictly forbidden to increase the purchases with a view to depriving the peasants of all surpluses, although formerly an increase of the levies by the authorities had been favoured. If, after the purchases had been made in full, certain surpluses remained with the peasants, the latter were entitled to put them on the market at free prices. Thus, after long years of relentless suppression, free market trading in agricultural products was once more permitted.

The Soviet Government favours the development of private live-stock farming among the members of the collectives ; it even favours the development of private market-gardening among the industrial workers, and has to this extent overcome its fears of a *petit-bourgeois* degeneration of the proletariat.

As had happened before under the N.E.P., these measures effected other spheres of economic life. By a government decision of July 23rd, 1932, the handicrafts co-operatives were no longer obliged to deliver their products to the Central Co-operatives at fixed prices ; they were empowered to sell them on the free market. They were also permitted to buy raw material independently subject to the condition that they did not compete with the large-scale state industry. Even the severe pressure which had burdened the individual handworker was somewhat lightened. In order to induce the peasants to put their surpluses on the market the government instructed the heavy industry to produce and market not only rails, locomotives and tractors, but also certain quantities of goods for the immediate consumption of the general public (" Širpotreb ").

In spite of certain similarities, we must not forget the profound difference which exists between this development since the summer of 1932, and that which took place under the N.E.P. The difference lies in the fact, that private trade was not only not permitted, but most vigorously suppressed. The producer had either to deal directly with the consumer or to sell his products to the state organisations. The latter agreed among themselves to purchase such products at " conventional " prices. This fact for its part was also bound to have its effect on the organisation of trade.

Even under the N.E.P. there had been in Soviet Russia not one but two systems of retail trading, with two separate price ranges. The co-operative and state shops usually sold their goods at more or less fixed prices and in an assortment which little suited the needs of their customers, while in private trade goods were sold at higher, fluctuating prices in an assortment which more nearly corresponded to the requirements of the purchasers. In the first years of the N.E.P. the price differences were slight; in 1923–4 about 11 per cent.[1] But as state trade, with its scanty selection of commodities, gradually drove out private trade, the difference between the price ranges widened, and in 1926–7 reached 35 per cent. The break up of the N.E.P. system led to a complete divorce of the fixed from the fluctuating prices. Soon after the Five Year Plan came into force private trade was almost entirely eliminated, and degenerated into an illicit traffic of very little economic significance. Thus in the second year of the Five Year period the system of uniform fixed prices was introduced.

But the increasing "commodity famine" proved to be a strong temptation to the government to win certain supplementary profits. Since 1930 only workers and employees of large-scale industry were permitted to receive their rations at low prices from the normal stock of goods in the so-called closed distribution centres. All other citizens who still possessed the right of membership in the co-operatives obtained their rations from other co-operative shops at considerably higher prices. People of bourgeois descent who were deprived of civil rights had to resort to what remained of private trade, and unless they received support from abroad they starved (permission to leave Russia is not granted). In 1930 a theory was propounded in the economic literature of the time to the effect that the rouble possessed no uniform value in Russia: the value of the rouble according to this view depended upon the class of the man to whom it belonged.

[1] *Wirtschaftsbulletin des Konjunkturinstituts*, 1927, Nos. 11–12, p. 17.

At the end of 1930 the Soviet Government recognised the possibility of making a certain break in the socialist system of distribution. "Torgsin" shops were opened in which goods were not rationed, but in which only foreign currencies or gold were accepted. In 1931 a more important step was taken in this direction : "commercial" shops were established in which goods were sold at very high prices for Russian money. Since 1932 it had been possible to buy agricultural products at "conventional" prices, and this provided a stimulus for extending the network of "commercial" shops ; in such shops the agricultural products bought at "conventional" prices are sold. Since 1933, moreover, an increasing share of manufactured goods have been distributed through these shops.

The differences between the prices of the different trading systems are very great. But the prices are seldom published. Professor Prokopovič's Economic Bureau—working on the basis of a price list in force in the Moscow District on the 1st of August, 1932—reckoned that the average index figure for twelve kinds of goods obtained from the standard sources of supply was 307 (1913 = 100) while in 1927–8 the retail index figure for the whole country amounted to 207.[1] The index figure for the commercial sources of supply was calculated by the bureau to be 1196. At the same time the average index figure for the prices offered by the government to the peasants for the expropriated grain remained at 150.[2] The free prices paid on the market to peasants by consumers for agricultural products are considerably higher even than those ruling in the commercial shops.

[1] "Control-figures" for the year 1928–9, p. 501.

[2] Prokopovič's Bulletin, No. 104, May 1933, pp. 8–9.

The development of the commercial shops provided the Soviet Government with an important new means of obtaining possession of the money surpluses which accumulated with the people and so mitigating the "commodity famine". (Hitherto the government had attempted to extract such surpluses by means of forced loans.) This new method, however, was to a certain extent in conflict with the nature of the Soviet Planned Economy. For a long time money wages in Soviet Russia had been sharply differentiated; yet in spite of this the differences between real wages had been insignificant, for wages consisted mainly of rations and not much could be obtained for the money which remained over. This state of affairs, approximating to communistic equality, was appropriate to conditions ruling under an economic system which was hardly capable of providing the consumers with the bare essentials of life. The development of trade on the market and in the shops—which in itself was a more efficient method of distributing goods than that of socialism—afforded to the differentiation of money wages a real significance. Rations were reduced and the markets and commercial shops were only open to those in possession of money. This, necessarily, affected the workers' interest in obtaining an increase of money wages. They exerted a certain pressure on the managers of industry, and in the last two years of the Five Year period the increase of money wages was more rapid than had been foreseen. Thus, in the iron industry in 1931, wages increased by 15·7 per cent over the preceding year, and in 1932 actually by 29·8 per cent over 1931. Altogether the wages of industrial workers increased by 70 per cent during the Five Year period,[1]

[1] *Results of the Completion of the Five Year Plan* . . ., p. 178.

though according to the plan they should only have increased by 47 per cent. As the improvement in the productivity of labour had been quite insignificant, the increase in money wages—even if it did not correspond to an increase in real wages—necessarily brought about a breach in the finance plan.

In 1933, therefore, a vigorous campaign against the raising of wages was announced. By a government decision of February 21st, 1933, the managers of industry were placed, in matters affecting the utilisation of the wages fund, under the strictest control of the higher courts. The government decision of December 3rd of the same year threatened managers with severe penalties if they increased wages on their own initiative.

Finance Commissar Grinko, in his speech to the 17th party conference (*Za industrializaciu* of Feb. 9, 1934) declared that a reduction of 1½ mlrd. roubles had been accomplished in 1933. If this is correct (statements as to the quantity of money have not been published), then it is hardly to be doubted that this successful step in the direction of an ordered currency—the first in a succession of years characterised by large money issues—could only have been achieved by developing the activity of the commercial shops. But commercial trade is in essential conflict with a planned economy which seeks to make great investments and which must, therefore, postpone satisfying the needs of the people. In a planned economy such as this any serious differentiation of real wages can hardly be supported.

In the fact that the peasants were permitted to sell, with formal freedom, the surpluses remaining with them after the government levies had been met; in the fact that the demands of home industry had to a certain extent been gratified; in the favour bestowed upon live-stock farming by individual peasants and upon the market-gardening of industrial workers; in all this we see an attempt at the end of the Five Year period to build a superstructure over and above the grandiose but clumsily planned economy. The planned economy had at once proved itself incapable of satisfying the needs of the people; the superstructure was a private economy on a modest scale. But the inner contradiction between the rigidly organised planned economy and these institutions of a free economic system makes the prospects of any successful development of the latter very questionable. The scope of private enterprise is confined within very narrow limits, and lacks any security in law. These institutions constitute something which, if of limited extent, is foreign to a system founded upon complete centralisation.

F. The Second Five Year Plan

Although the Soviet Government is attempting to convert Russia as quickly as possible into an industrial country, and asserts that with the fulfilment of the Five Year Plan this task has already been accomplished, the economic position of the country remains absolutely dependent on the grain harvest. So it was before the Five Year Plan and so it remains now that the plan is supposed to have been carried out. The famine of 1932–3 has proved that Soviet Russia in spite of all its industrial "gigantics" is not in a position to obtain grain for its suffering people by selling the products of its grandly conceived industry—even though grain is the cheapest commodity on the world market.

The famines which resulted from its economic policy exercised a somewhat depressing effect upon the spirits of the Bolshevists. Under their influence the government restricted its plans and sought to make certain compromises with private enterprise; for private enterprise at least understood, in one way or another, how to satisfy the immediate needs of the people. In the same way the catastrophic famine of 1921–2 induced Lenin to announce the N.E.P. "seriously and for a long time". Similarly the famines of 1932 and 1933 induced the communists to resuscitate certain rudiments of private trade and to postpone the second Five Year Plan. But good harvests come again, famine is soon forgotten and the party turns once more to its grandiose plans. In just the same way the excellent harvests of 1925 and 1926 led to the abandonment of the N.E.P. system, and the good harvest of 1930 resulted in a return to forcible collectivisation. The comparatively good grain harvest of 1933 had similar consequences. There is no doubt that this good harvest was entirely due to the excellent weather conditions, for in 1933 there was a further decline in live-stock farming and the fields were on that account badly tilled and inadequately manured. The yield per unit of land under intensive cultivation, where careful attention is required, remained low even in 1933. But abundant rains ensure a good grain harvest in the Steppes, however badly the fields are cultivated, and in this region no manuring at all is required.

The good grain harvest of 1933 induced a more cheerful mood in the party. Communists ascribed the satisfactory results to their wise policy, and particularly to the discipline imposed upon the peasants by the newly formed sections of the G.P.U. in the country. Consequently the second Five Year Plan was put on the agenda by the Party Congress of January-February 1934. Owing to the confused state of the currency this plan could not be worked out in detail, as was the first. It was simply announced in programme speeches by the communist leaders, and in the plans themselves there are numerous contradictions.

The plans are not so extravagant as the outline of January 1932 suggested, but they are nevertheless very strained. A further enormous expansion of the most important branches of heavy industry is proposed, with a view to doubling and even trebling their output in five years. The peasantry must be collectivised to the last man. Thus, it is thought, the final construction of a classless society will be possible. Naturally the plans promise a very considerable improvement in the standard of living. The central feature of the whole plan is the development of the Magnitogorsk-Kuzneck combine; on account of the great distances involved this task is the most difficult and expensive, but out of military considerations Stalin lays the greatest emphasis upon it.

In the first Five Year period 50·5 mlrd. roubles were invested in the socialised sector of society. In the second period 133·4 mlrd. roubles are to be invested. The plan again expects that the state enterprises, on account of their high productivity, will furnish the funds necessary for the investments.

It is very clear—and indeed it was proved by experience under the Five Year Plan—that great investments result in the depression of the people's standard of living to the lowest level. All the resources of the economic system will be strained for the sake of these new investments, the profitability of which is by no means assured. Under such conditions there can hardly be room for the rudiments of a private economy, and after the announcement of the second Five Year Plan their prospects are not favourable. Although the plan would like to abolish the primitive forms of a force-economy, and especially the distribution of consumption goods in rations, it is difficult to believe in the possibility of ridding the system of these primitive and—even to the communists—abhorrent institutions.

IV

THE RESULTS OF THE SOVIET RUSSIAN PLANNED ECONOMY AND THEIR VALUATION

A. The Investments

THE result of the Five Year Plan was that great investments were made in a poor country, in a country which had not yet had time to recover from the devastation of foreign war, social revolution and civil war. Without the technical assistance of capitalist countries the great industrial building projects could not have been carried out; but while before the war foreign capital played a very important part in the development of Russian industry, financial assistance from abroad was now quite modest.[1] The great investments, therefore, were made out of the resources of a poverty-stricken country. Hence we may consider the specific achievement of the planned economy to be the fact that it compelled a poor nation to make great savings. Anything of the sort would have been impossible in a market economy.

In the absence of statistical data it is impossible to compute accurately the investments made. But there can be no doubt that it was not possible to get so much out of the national income as the Five Year Plan con-

[1] According to Memorandum No. 4 of the Birmingham Bureau (p. 10), Soviet Russia's total foreign debts up to October 1, 1931, amounted to 1,205 mill. roubles.

templated. According to the Five Year Plan, the investments were to amount to 64·5 mlrd. roubles; according to the calculations of the Gosplan, they did amount to 60 mlrd. roubles.[1] But these figures are hardly comparable, for at the end of the Five Year period the quantity of money was nearly twice as great as it should have been according to the plan. Although, thanks to the planned economy, the inflation did not have its full effect upon the prices of building materials, it was in any case impossible to achieve the reduction of such prices that was planned. Moreover, building does not depend exclusively upon goods whose prices were planned; there was, for example, much complaint in the Soviet Press about the exorbitant costs of road transport which greatly increased the cost of building.

According to the Gosplan's report, instead of the 17·6 mlrd. roubles which were contemplated, only 7·5 mlrd. roubles were invested in the private sector of society; while in the socialised sector 52·5 mlrd. roubles were invested instead of 46·9 mlrd. When we consider the intolerable situation of the individual peasantry and private enterprise, it is difficult to imagine what this investment of 7·5 mlrd. roubles amounted to; in the report these figures are given without any kind of details. The Gosplan's report points out with satisfaction that the investments into the socialised sector of society were somewhat greater (by 12 per cent) than were provided for by the estimates in the Five Year Plan. Accordingly the report considers that "the Five Year Plan has been surpassed in its most important and decisive part, and this has assured that the work of technical reconstruction,

[1] See the Gosplan Report, *Results of the Completion of the first Five Year Plan . . .* (Russian), p. 254.

as set forth in the plan, will be surpassed both in range and degree ". Here the writers of the report completely ignore the fact that money has depreciated and that the building operations did not proceed with anything like the orderly precision that was called for. The effect of these two facts was that the building index was 25 per cent higher in 1932 than in 1928 whereas according to the Five Year Plan it should have been 40 per cent lower ;[1] and this means that in the last year of the Five Year period 200 roubles spent on building yielded hardly as much as 100 roubles should, according to the plan, have yielded. Thus it is clear that even in the socialised sector the investments produced much less than they should have done according to the plan.

It must also be remembered that the Five Year Plan assumes that building projects commenced are brought to completion. This, however, it was by no means possible to achieve. According to the Gosplan's report (p. 40), in the Five Year period the total capital invested in uncompleted building works increased by 12 mlrd. roubles ; it amounted, that is, to nearly a quarter (22·9 per cent) of the capital invested in the socialised sector. In the case of industrial buildings, the position was still worse ; for example in the iron industry 3 mlrd. roubles were invested (instead of the 2,165 millions contemplated by the Five Year Plan) while buildings actually put into use were valued at only 1½ mlrd. roubles.[2] So that for this reason also the results of the building works were much more modest than the plan had foreseen.

[1] See report on the conference of Building Managers in *Ekonom. Žizn'* of January 17, 1933.

[2] See speech by Rudzutak, president of the Central Control Commission, etc., at the 17th congress (*Za industrializaciu* of February 5, 1934).

But the degree in which the investments were carried out was very different in different branches of industry. In the heavy industry investments of 14·7 mlrd. roubles were specified by the plan ; actually 21·3 mlrd. roubles were invested—44·9 per cent more. As against this, while the investments into all other branches of economic activity should have amounted to 49·8 mlrd. roubles, the actual figure was 38·7 mlrd. roubles or 22 per cent less ; and this includes the 7·5 mlrd. roubles said to have been invested in the private sector. For the reasons we have given, even in the sphere of heavy industry the building operations did not reach the figures foreseen in the Five Year Plan ; in this department indeed, the proportion of building works not brought to completion was especially high. Nevertheless, in this sphere of industry the plans were carried out to a greater extent than elsewhere. From the very beginning the plan was one-sidedly conceived, for the investments it proposed to make into heavy industry were too great in comparison with those proposed for the other branches of the economic system. In the actual execution of the plan this one-sidedness was not relieved but actually intensified, and this partly explains the distortions under which the Russian people suffer so much.

The specific feature of the Russian economic development under the Five Year Plan, therefore, was not only that great investments were made in a poor country, but also that these investments were directed into the production goods industry ; thus the capital investments took the longest way round, whereas in a poor country they usually take the shorter ways. Only under a planned economy could the investments take such a form in the given circumstances.

The principal aim of the Five Year Plan was the development of a great heavy industry, and in general it must be recognised that this aim was achieved. Even if many factories were not completed by the end of the period, and building had to be continued during the following years, this fact is not of decisive significance in estimating the results of the Five Year Plan. If the Soviet Government is especially concerned to prove that the plan was completely carried out in the Five Year period, its motives are propagandist. From the scientific point of view the fact that the execution of the plan took not four and a quarter years, but longer, cannot be said to compromise the Russian planned economy. What is problematical in the Russian system lies elsewhere.

The superficial successes achieved in the construction of the heavy industry are remarkable. The basic supply of energy to the economic system was expanded by the construction of a series of power stations. New coalfields were developed outside the Donetz basin, in particular the enormous coalfield of Kuzneck (Western Siberia); deposits of coal in the Urals, of brown coal near Moscow and of peat, were exploited. This made it possible to decentralise industry without, at least proportionally, increasing the dependence of industry on coal supplies from the Donetz basin. The iron industry showed a notable expansion; here most emphasis was laid upon the development, on a great scale, of the Magnitogorsk-Kuzneck combine. According to the Five Year Plan, the capacity of blast furnaces in operation was to increase from 20,000 cubic metres to 36,800 cubic metres or 84 per cent and the areas covered by Martin furnaces [1] from 4,630 square metres

[1] Gosplan Report, pp. 108, 109.

to 6,421 square metres, or 39 per cent. The engineering industry was developed on an especially imposing scale; there hardly remain machines so complex that they cannot be built in Russia. After the U.S.A., Russia has the greatest tractor industry in the world, whereas before the Five Year Plan the Russian production of tractors was quite insignificant. A great new chemical industry, hardly existent before the war, has grown up. According to the calculations of Professor Prokopovič, the value of the original capital of Russian industry amounted in 1928 to 3,700 mill. roubles in pre-war prices, while at the end of the Five Year Plan it amounted to 8,134 mill. roubles;[1] thus capital increased by 120 per cent. In spite of all the reservations which have to be made in connection with such computations, these figures do give an idea of the magnitude of the capital investments into industry.

B. Industrial Production

The increase in industrial production could not reflect the energy displayed in building activity, for, as we have shown, a considerable percentage of the new buildings were not completed by the end of the Five Year period. According to the Gosplan's report, industrial production was to increase by 133·3 per cent under the Five Year Plan, and the plan was 93·7 per cent accomplished. No reliance can be placed upon these figures, which are based on prices; such calculations belong to the sphere of that "statistical demagogy" which is a feature of all reports issued in Soviet Russia under the Five Year

[1] Prokopovič, *The Planning Scheme and the Results of the Five Year Plan*, with preface by P. N. Miliukov. Paris, 1934, p. 95.

Plan. The authorities want to show, for the benefit of foreign countries, the successes achieved by the planned economy; and it is possible to prove anything by manipulating prices in an economy in which there is no ordered currency and no regular market business. We may obtain a more objective view of the results of the Five Year Plan in the sphere of industrial production if we express the development not in money-values but in actual quantities—though even here the fluctuating quality of the goods produced is an incalculable factor.

On the opposite page we tabulate certain figures relating to production in the most important branches of heavy industry.[1]

The figures bear witness to a very considerable expansion in heavy industry; in most branches production was doubled and in many it was more than doubled. Important exceptions, however, were two branches of heavy industry: the increase in steel production was 40 per cent and of sheet iron only 26 per cent.

In spite of the progress made by heavy industry, the plan was more or less fulfilled only in the fuel-producing industry. Yet even here the success was only superficial; in reality the shortage of coal was very acute under the Five Year Plan, for the demand for coal was much greater than the plan had estimated. There were two reasons for this larger demand. In the first place the plan reckoned on increasing the efficiency of coal to such an extent that 30 per cent of it would be saved, whereas such savings were in no way realised. Secondly, the rapid construction of industry in the East greatly

[1] Production figures for the year 1927–8 and Plan figures for the year 1932–3 are taken from *The Five Year Plan* . . ., vol. ii, pt. I, pp. 254–7; the Completion figures from the Gosplan, pp. 64–126.

Industries.	Units.	Production 1927–8.	Production 1932.	1932 in percentage of 1927–8.	1932 according to Five Year Plan.	Percentage fulfilment of Five Year Plan.
Production of Electric Power	Million K.W. hours	5,000	13,100	262	22,000	60
Fuel Industries:						
Coal . . .	Million tons	35·4	64·4	179	75	86
Crude oil . .	ditto	11·7	22·2	190	21·7	102
Peat . . .	ditto	5·4	13·85	257	12·3	112
Iron Industry:						
Pig Iron . .	ditto	3·3	6·2	189	10	62
Steel . . .	ditto	4·2	5·9	140	10·4	57
Rolled Iron .	ditto	3·4	4·2	126	8	52·5
Copper . .	Thousand tons	28·3	46·7	165	84·7	55
Building Materials:						
Cement . .	Million barrels	11·9	22·5	189	41	52
Bricks . . .	Milliard pieces	1·78	4·8	269	9·3	52
Sawn Timber	Million cubic metres	11·55	22·2	192	42·5	55
Chemical Industries:						
Superphosphate	Thousand tons	150	612	408	3,400	18
Nitric Acid .	ditto	208	495	238	1,450	34

increased the demand for coal by the railways. For this reason the control-figures [1] for 1932 require a production of 90 mill. tons instead of 75 mill. tons; and in comparison with this increased figure, the planned coal

[1] All the planned figures are now called control-figures.

production was only 71·5 per cent achieved. In the three most important departments of the heavy industry—the production of electricity, metals and building materials—a 50–60 per cent fulfilment of the plans was attained; in chemical industry the percentage was much lower still.

Somewhat in contrast to the results achieved by all these departments of heavy industry, production in engineering is said to have been enormous. In this sphere the Soviet economic system was trying to make itself self-sufficient, and indeed the serious reduction in the value of its exports made such self-sufficiency essential. The value of machines produced is said to have increased from 1,382 mill. roubles in 1928 to 5,330 mill. roubles in 1932, and if one accepts the prices underlying these calculations, then the engineering industry grew to four times its size and the plan was surpassed by 22 per cent. Yet in the production of agricultural machines—for which the demand had grown most of all owing to the collectivisation of the peasant farms—the plan was far from being carried out. The expansion of the engineering industry demanded great sacrifices from the country. The fact that production in the iron industry had fallen short necessitated the import of 3·2 mill. tons of iron, valued at 305·7 mill. roubles, in the four years 1929–32. The iron was applied quite one-sidedly to the engineering industry, while in agriculture, communal trading and in house building the consumption of iron not only did not increase but actually had to be curtailed.[1]

In evaluating this considerable expansion of heavy

[1] See my article, "Die russische Eisenindustrie" ("The Russian Iron Industry") in *Der deutsche Volkswirt* of June 16, 1933, p. 1058.

industry we must remember that Russia is still a young country industrially. In such a country, assuming favourable trading conditions, industrial development can proceed at a much more rapid pace than in a country which has long been industrialised. Thus in the three years from 1910 to 1913, the production of coal rose from 25·0 to 36·2 mill. tons, of pig iron from 3·1 to 4·8 mill. tons and of copper from 22·3 to 33·8 thousand tons—increases of 45 per cent, 57 per cent and 51 per cent respectively.[1]

In the Gosplan's report on the Five Year Plan it is pointed out that production in heavy industry (Group A) increased by 172·7 per cent; in comparison with this enormous expansion that of light industry (Group B) is more modest, though it is still sufficiently imposing at 101·2 per cent. The report gives a fair amount of data—in terms of goods—with regard to the quantitative development of the heavy industry; but with regard to the quantitative development of light industry it prefers to remain silent, and the entire Russian Press refrains from quoting the relevant figures. In the table on page 204 we give details regarding the five most important branches of light industry; these particulars are quoted from the speech of Molotov, Chairman of People's Commissars of the Union, at the 17th party Congress.[2]

According to these figures, no progress was made in the two most important textile industries. The reason for this failure was the fact that the Soviet Government,

[1] *The Economic System in the year 1913*, Finance Ministry, published at the office of the *Vestnik finansov* and the *Torgovo-promyšlennaia gazeta*, Petrograd, 1914, pp. 305, 361, 397. The figures refer to Russia's former territory.

[2] *Za industrializaciu* of February 6, 1934.

Industries.	Units.	Production 1927–8	Production 1932	1932 in percentage of 1927–8.	1932–3 according to Five Year Plan.	Percentage fulfilment of Five Year Plan.
Cotton Materials	Million metres	2,742	2,720	99	4,700	58
Woollen Materials	ditto	96·6	91·3	94·5	270	35
Glass . . .	Thousand tons	320	396·4	124	800	49·5
Leather Shoes	Million pairs	23	81·9	356	80	102
Preserved Food	Million tins	90	716	796	650	110

in order to increase the imports of mechanical equipment, suspended all foreign buying of cotton and wool; but an increase in the domestic production of raw material occurred only in the case of cotton, and that to an inadequate extent. The increase in glass production was small, and the plan was only performed to the extent of 50 per cent. The position with regard to the production of leather shoes and preserved food seems to be better. Yet these successes give rise to certain doubts. The enormous development of the nationalised shoe industry was achieved through the simultaneous destruction, by administrative measures, of the home industry. Now there can be no question that products of the home industry were both much more solid and much more in accordance with the requirements of the customers than were those of the nationalised industry, and, moreover, they were much better distributed. As for the canning industry, this is almost entirely a creation of the Soviet Government. The latter concentrates in its hands large stocks of perishable foodstuffs which it does not know how properly to distribute ; the Soviet Press is filled with reports about vast quantities of such goods having been spoilt. A percentage of them are converted into preserves of very indifferent quality. Both in the case of shoes and preserved food we are indeed witnessing an important advance in socialist industry, which the government values highly. But this progress of socialism, which for the Soviet Government is an end in itself, is not as yet the same thing as economic progress. On the contrary, the requirements of consumers are satisfied not better, but worse.

The quantitative expansion of industrial production, as we have already said, is to a large extent set off by the fall in the quality of the goods produced. The mass production of waste commodities is not an exceptional thing in Russia, but quite a normal process. And, what is more, these unsaleable products are valued at normal prices. The Soviet Press is literally flooded with complaints about the bad quality of industrial products. Out of innumerable examples we may quote the following, taken as it is from a newspaper thoroughly competent to speak on this question : [1]

> The percentage of inferior products is enormous. . . . There is no branch of light industry which can boast of an inconsiderable percentage of spoiled and unsaleable goods. For example, in the hosiery industry the percentage of waste amounts to 37–50 per cent. Individual trusts and factories give quite extraordinary figures—80–90 per cent.

The newspaper comments here that even goods which are accepted as standard are often of low quality. Even

[1] " Light Industries," of June 4 and 23, 1933. Quoted from the Prokopovič Bulletin of May 1933, p. 11.

in heavy industry—in so far as the quality is not determined by nature—the state of affairs is no better than in light industry.

In Russia hardly anything is more widely discussed than the quality of goods. Innumerable committees have been set up to put a stop to the production of goods of low quality. At last, on December 8th, 1933, a government decision was taken by which the managerial personnel of the factories producing inferior goods were to be held criminally responsible. And yet no improvement is to be observed. This goes to prove that such a state of affairs is fundamental to a socialist planned economy. The decisive cause is not merely the over-rapid development which took place under the Five Year Plan, but also the monopoly position held by Soviet industry, and the " commodity famine " ; for where there is an absolute scarcity of goods people are willing and are often compelled to take what is offered without considering quality. In the few cases where goods are designed for foreign markets attention is paid to quality ; then even Soviet industry knows how to make serviceable goods.

The Five Year Plan was based upon the notion that by " fertilising " labour with abundant capital and by transplanting the most up-to-date technical methods on to Russian soil, an enormous increase in the productivity of labour could be achieved. In five years this productivity was to increase by 110 per cent. Actually, however, hardly any improvement took place. Although the production plan was not carried out either quantitatively or qualitatively, the personnel, in all spheres of economic life increased at a much more rapid pace than had been foreseen. According to the Five

Year Plan, the number of workers and employees in the large-scale industries was to increase by 30·5 per cent, from 3,126 thousand to 4,080·1 thousand. In fact the figures in 1932 were 6,311·1 thousand, so that the number of employees had doubled.[1] Yet officially it is asserted that the productivity of labour increased by 41 per cent.[2] How the Gosplan arrived at this result, which is in contradiction to the facts, remains obscure. According to the calculations of Professor Prokopovič, the productivity of labour has increased as to its gross yield by 9·1 per cent and as to its net yield by 5·3 per cent.[3]

In all such calculations there is a great deal that is problematical. More illuminating are comparisons between the productivity of labour in Soviet Russia and abroad, as expressed in terms of goods and confined to definite industries. In the Donetz basin production per shift in 1931 was 0·61 tons; in England in 1929 1·2 tons; in the Ruhr 1·53 tons, and in the U.S.A., in 1929—4·85 tons. In the blast-furnace plants of the Southern area of the U.S.S.R. the production of pig iron per worker in 1930 was 24 tons per month; in the U.S.A. in 1927 it was 140 tons. In the U.S.S.R. the monthly production of steel per worker was 17 tons; in Germany, in 1927, 47 tons.[4] From these figures it is evident that the productivity of labour in Soviet Russia, in spite of the most modern machinery, lags far behind the productivity of labour in other countries.

[1] Gosplan Report, p. 173.
[2] *Ibid.*, p. 176.
[3] *The Planning Scheme, etc.* (Russian), p. 78.
[4] *Ekonom. Žizn'*, September 2 and 30, 1932, quoted from *Auhagen*, p. 24.

C. Agricultural Production

Whatever one's estimate of the achievement of Russian large-scale industry, its rapid expansion cannot be questioned. The case of agriculture under the Five Year Plan was very different. The most dangerous feature of the Russian economic situation on the eve of the introduction of the Five Year Plan was the lag in grain production. In 1928, land under grain amounted to 0·62 ha. per head of the population, as against 0·74 ha. in 1930—i.e. the area per head was less by 16 per cent at the earlier date ; the total area under grain in 1928 amounted to 94·7 mill. ha. as against 102·7 mill. ha. in 1930—i.e. it was less by 8 mill. ha.[1] Agricultural statistics in Soviet Russia are least reliable of all, but even they are sufficient to indicate that the increase in the area of land under grain was inadequate in 1932. 99·7 mill. ha. were harvested, which was still 3 mill. ha. less than before the war.[2] And not only was the land under cultivation less than before the war, but the average amount of grain harvested from each unit of land was less than before the war : it was reckoned at 7·5 dz. per ha. for the five years 1928–32, as against 8·25 dz. per ha. for the five years before the war.[3] Thus the average grain

[1] Control-figures for the year 1928–9, pp. 408–11.

[2] The Gosplan Report on the Completion of the Five Year Plan suddenly fixes the figure for the grain area under cultivation in the year 1913 in Russian territory (as it is to-day) at 94·4 mill. hectares. This new figure, which contradicts the official estimate, rests on no foundation and appears to be intended to disguise somewhat the unfavourable situation of the grain industry.

[3] The first figure is taken from the lecture given by Molotov, president of the People's Commissars (*Za industrializaciu* of January 6, 1934) ; the second, from the calculations of the celebrated Russian statistician Von Groman in his article, " Grain Production and Export in the U.S.S.R." (*Encyclopædia of Soviet Exports*), Berlin, 1928, vol. i, p. 238.

harvest was lower under the Five Year Plan than before the war. If we remember that the population at the end of the Five Year Plan was at least 15 per cent greater than before the war, and that exports before the war took about 16 per cent of the net harvest, then it is clear that Russia to-day is not in a position—even without exporting—to consume as much grain per head as before the war; and even in those days the consumption of grain was not particularly high.[1] In such circumstance the export of grain in 1931 and 1932, amounting altogether to 10·7 mill. tons, was not justified, and its effect was catastrophic.

The fact that Russia is now no longer in possession of grain surpluses for shipment abroad is of ominous significance for her balance of trade, for before the war the value of Russian grain sent to foreign countries amounted to nearly half of her exports.

In the interest of industrialisation the Soviet Government sought to extend the area of land devoted to "technical" crops; that is, those crops which provide industry with raw material, such as sugar beet in the North Ukraine, cotton in Turkestan, flax in the North, sunflowers in the South-east, and so on. While before the war only 4·55 mill. ha. were devoted to "technical" crops, areas under such cultivation amounted to 8·6 mill. ha. in 1928 and to 14·8 mill. ha. in 1932. But the technical crops call for very careful attention, and mechanisation, upon which the Soviet Government bases all its hopes, could not achieve very much here. The

[1] According to the calculations of the Birmingham Bureau, Memorandum 8, Table III, the net yield per head of the population in the year 1913 was 4·9 dz. and the average of the years 1928–9 to 1932–3 only 3·9 dz., that is, about 20 per cent less.

result was that the rapid increase of acreage under cultivation was accompanied by a sharp further decrease in the crops harvested per unit of land ; and even before the yield per unit was not particularly high. The following details make the position clear :[1]

Crops.	Harvests in Dz. per hectare.			Harvests of the years 1930–3 in percentage of the years 1909–13.
	1909–13.	1925–9.	1930–3.	
Cotton	3·8	2·6	2·1	55
Flax	4·0	2·4	2·0	50
Sugar Beet	160·7	127·8	82·2	51
Sunflowers	10·7 *	6·1	6·3	56

* Refers to 1913 only.

The table shows that the crops harvested per unit of land to-day amount to only half what they did before the war. Owing to the enormous increase in the area of land under cultivation there was, in spite of this, an increase in the gross harvests of most of the technical crops ; sugar beet, of which the gross harvests fluctuate widely, is an exception, and the pre-war average was hardly attained even from a cultivated area nearly twice as great as before the war. The policy of supplanting grain in favour of technical crops—which was often, as in the case of the extension of cotton-growing in Turkestan, enforced by heavy pressure from the government—loses any economic justification when such crops are so meagre and uncertain. At last the Soviet Govern-

[1] These numbers are calculated from the Prokopovič Bulletin, No. 100, of November-December 1932 and supplemented by statements in Stalin's speech at the 17th Congress (*Za industrializaciu* of January 28, 1934).

ment had to recognise the fact, and in 1931 the area of land devoted to technical crops was reduced to 11·45 mill. ha.

In order to give a picture of the Russian live-stock situation it is only necessary to quote the following table. It is taken from Stalin's speech to the 17th party congress, and is of especial interest as the figures for 1933 are published here for the first time.[1]

LIVE STOCK IN U.S.S.R. IN MILLIONS OF HEAD

	1916.	1929.	1930.	1931.	1932.	1933.	1933 in percentage of 1929.
Horses . . .	35·1	34·0	30·2	26·2	19·6	16·6	48·8
Cattle . . .	58·9	68·1	52·5	47·9	40·7	38·6	56·7
Sheep . . .	115·2	147·2	108·8	77·7	52·1	50·6	34·4
Pigs	20·3	20·9	13·6	14·4	11·6	12·2	58·6

The figures for 1929 show that live-stock farming had experienced a very considerable recovery under the New Economic Policy. But since that year the number of horses has fallen by a half, of cattle by nearly a half, of sheep by two-thirds and of pigs by two-fifths. The reduction in the quantity of live stock in 1930 and 1931 may be regarded as the direct result of compulsory collectivisation; the peasants were unwilling to hand over their beasts to the collectives and preferred to slaughter them. But the fact that the diminution continued during the two following years shows that the conditions of socialist agriculture are unfavourable to live stock breeding. The effects of the great levies were also of decisive importance. After the peasants had

[1] *Za industrializaciu*, January 28, 1934.

delivered the grain they had hardly sufficient for themselves, and none was available for use as fodder.

Live stock is the farmers' most valuable form of capital, and this catastrophic decline determines the general position of Russian agriculture. We have to consider a disastrous fall in available tractive power; for there can be no question of replacing draught animals with tractors, although communists imagined this to be possible quite recently. It has been estimated that Russian agriculture possessed 25·2 mill. draught horses in 1929 and 12·3 mill. in 1933, i.e. 12·9 mill. less.[1] Moreover, the numbers of draught oxen, estimated at 4·6 mill. head in 1929 fell to 2 mill. At best the tractors can take the place of 4 mill. horses.[2] Altogether we arrive at a reduction of tractive power,[3] in terms of horses, from 28·3 mill. in 1929 to 17·6 mill. in 1933, i.e. by more than a third. In 1932 the Russian tractor factories produced 45 thousand tractors. Even if it were found possible considerably to increase their productivity in subsequent years, the machines wear out so rapidly that we can only look for a very slow increase in the total number. Thus, to replenish the supply of horses is the vital problem for Russian agriculture, and it is now recognised as such by the Soviet Government in spite of the latter's enthusiasm for mechanical farming.

Moreover, the decline in stock-breeding threatens Russian agriculture from another direction. In the Steppe regions the fields require no manure, but in the northern black earth region good harvests cannot

[1] Prokopovič Bulletin, No. 111, February-March 1934, p. 14.

[2] *The Five Year Plan* . . ., vol. ii, pt. I, pp. 274–5.

[3] Counting three oxen as equivalent to two horses.

be obtained without it. As for the cold northern half of European Russia, there the productivity of the land is absolutely dependent upon animal manure, just as it is, for example, in Germany ; it is possible to supplement animal manures with mineral fertilisers, but not to replace them. The revival of stock-raising is a slow process, and the second Five Year Plan, which is conceived in a thoroughly optimistic spirit raises no hopes of the task being accomplished within the time set. This means that compulsory collectivisation has resulted in a long period of sickness for Russian agriculture.

D. The Industrialisation of the Land

Russia is a great continental country. It was an agricultural country, and so far as we can see into the future no fundamental change is possible in this connection. Russia's very considerable natural resources permit of industrial development, and if the country is to make economic progress such development is indispensable. But Russian industry must be supported by the internal market. It might take as a pattern the United States, whose vast industry produces for the domestic market and only to a quite modest extent for abroad. Germany, whose industry is very dependent upon foreign trade, is a less appropriate model, and least of all is England. Under the pressure of the world crisis even Germany and England have sought to increase the significance of the home market from the point of view of industry.

In Russia we see the grafting on to the economic system of a large-scale heavy industry which the people, owing to the precipitate rate of the general development, does not in the least know how to manage : at the same time we see the main support of Russian economic life being undermined. This from the economic point of view is not progress but the greatest possible blunder. In a market economy, where the economic life obeys laws of its own, a state of affairs such as this could never come about ; but under a planned economy, as the example shows, this pathological development is possible.

As the Soviet Government recognises only absolute values (capitalism is bad, socialism is good, simple technique is bad, complicated technique is good, and so on) even this form of economic degeneration is glorified as industrialisation ; for an absolute value is ascribed to industrialisation. At the same time economic literature seeks to prove that this industrialisation has been carried much farther than is, in fact, the case.[1] Soviet writers point out with great satisfaction that while the productive value of the output of the production goods industry in 1928 was still 44·3 per cent

[1] It is calculated (see the Gosplan's Report, p. 14, and Stalin's speech of January 27, 1934, at the 17th Congress) that, of the gross yield of economic production in the year 1932, no more and no less than 70·9 per cent falls upon industry, and on the strength of this it is assumed that Soviet Russia has definitely become transformed into an industrial state. In discussing this question the low valuation of agricultural, in comparison with industrial products must be taken into account, and also the fact that in calculating the gross yield of industry, the value of many raw materials and semi-manufactured articles has been counted in several times over. The net production of industry formed, in the years 1928–32, 37 to 45 per cent of the gross production. (See A. Putilov, " The Problem of Industrial Economies ", *Planovoe Chozyaystvo*, 1932, pt. 5, p. 113.) The distribution of the net production at pre-war prices had shown that even now agriculture in spite of its decline, is a more valuable creative factor than industry. This is borne out by the fact that in the year 1932, 71·2 per cent of the population were supported by agriculture.

of the total value of all industrial products, in 1932 it was already 52·5 per cent. The composition of the goods produced by Russian industry approximated to that of Germany and England. As for the Russian engineering industry, its production is said to be one and a half times greater than that of Germany and England, of two countries that is, which provide the whole world with machinery. If industrialisation is not to be regarded as a thing valuable in itself, then it is precisely these last facts that give rise to the gravest doubts. In the rapid development of a production goods industry which supplies goods of low quality and is not controlled by the principle of profitability, there lie great perils. To illustrate these, let me quote the opinion of the Supreme Economic Council, which runs as follows :[1]

> On October 8th, 1929, the presiding body of the Supreme Economic Council was obliged to put on record that in a large number of branches of production, the quality of the goods manufactured has—to the disgrace of our trusts and managements—deteriorated to an extraordinary extent. The bad quality of the coal and iron forms one of the principal reasons for the fact that the production of iron has not kept up with the production programme. The extremely bad quality of the iron has made it impossible for industries working up iron to complete their production programme. With this is also connected the unsatisfactory state of the agricultural machine industry—a dangerous condition, inasmuch as it will result in the peasants being without tools and machines for the work of cultivation in the spring.

A production goods industry of this sort may become its own end and purpose ; and in fact we do get the

[1] *Za industrializaciu*, January 8, 1930.

impression that the great Russian production goods industry feeds, so to speak, upon itself.

E. The Economic Situation of the Masses

When we make a study of Soviet literature we receive the impression that all these buildings on so grand a scale are regarded as ends in themselves; the fact that they ought to serve the requirements of the people seems to have been forgotten.

Even under the New Economic Policy the conditions of the market were unfavourable to the peasants. But their exploitation by the socialist sector of society was restricted to a certain extent by the existence of private trading. After the catastrophe of 1921–2 was overcome the peasants did not experience famine, not even after the very poor harvest of 1924. Under the Five Year Plan the demands made upon the peasants by the Soviet Government grew enormously, and thanks to the methods of forcible expropriation, these demands were met. From the grain harvest of 1928 the Soviet Government took 14·7 per cent, and from the harvest of 1931, 32·9 per cent of the gross yield.[1] The purveyance of grain fell most heavily upon the southern areas, and the extent to which it was carried may be gathered from the following words of the *Ekonom. Žizn'* of August 18th, 1932: "For many of the collectives of the Rayons Voznesensk (Ukrainian Steppe) the grain acquisition plan embraced 80 per cent of the gross yield and in certain cases actually the entire gross yield. In many collectives of Gaue Vinnica and Kiev (Ukrainian Forest Steppe) the

[1] See further details in my article, " Russlands Getreideausfuhr *op. cit.*, October 1933, pp. 497–8.

acquisition plans embraced nearly the whole gross yield." But that was only printed after the great stocks of grain had been exported from the Ukrainian ports. In spite of the catastrophic decline in livestock farming, the acquisitions of animal products (with the exception of eggs) were not decreased but increased.[1] The export of foodstuffs for animals was not suspended. Thus the peasantry was plunged into the famine of 1932–3.

In estimating the effects of the Five Year Plan from the point of view of the workers, we must remember that their position before the collapse of the N.E.P. system was fairly favourable. According to the calculations of the Institute of Economic Research, individual real wages of the workers were higher in 1926–7 by 10–11 per cent than before the war, and if the income provided by socialised institutions (the social sections) is included, they were actually higher by a third.[2] At that time the not very numerous working class, which in every respect was favoured, had something to show for the revolution. Although under the Five Year Plan the Soviet Government sought with the aid of the great levies to secure the interests of the workers, it has not been successful. The state trading organisations did not know how to store the great levies properly. They did not understand how rightly to distribute them; a considerable percentage of them was exported in order to pay for the imports of machinery; and finally the produce obtained had to be divided between a rapidly growing number of workers and even of peasants (the latter having been compelled to extend the cultivation of technical crops at the expense of grain). After the

[1] Prokopovič Bulletin, No. 109, December 1933, p. 7.

[2] *Wirtschaftsbulletin des Konjunkturinstituts*, 1927, Nos. 11–12, p. 4.

first campaign to bring about compulsory collectivisation the market in animal products, which had formerly been still fairly active, disappeared. This was felt particularly by the workers. The famine which raged in the south in 1932–3 also fell heavily upon the town workers.

The living conditions of the workers are quite shocking. The revolution brought about the demolition of a considerable part of the available dwelling accommodation. On that account living conditions were very bad even before the Five Year Plan came into force. From particulars given in the Gosplan's report (pp. 186 and 253) it may be calculated that accommodation allotted to the town populations amounted to only 5·8 sq. m. per head, while in Soviet Russia 8·0 sq. m. was regarded as the minimum. In 1932 the average had fallen still further to 4·8 sq. m.[1]

Conditions, however, vary. More care is taken of the workers in the large cities, while the position is worse for those employed in mines and on buildings under construction. The latter are least satisfactorily provided for and housed.

> I must draw attention particularly to the incredibly bad living conditions. Up to the present not a single dwelling-house has been finished for the workers. The latter are lodged in provisional barracks where there is no water, where unspeakably dirty conditions prevail and where rain comes through the roof. Far too little attention is paid to the dwelling and living conditions of the workers. The dining-rooms are filthy. . . .

Such is the report of no less a personage than Ordžonikidze, the People's Commissar for heavy in-

[1] In the Gosplan Report (p. 186) only the increase of the dwelling areas is mentioned ; there is no calculation of the living space per inhabitant.

dustry, and his words relate not to some wretched slums but to the world-famous smelting-works of Magnitogorsk. Workers employed on many of the buildings under construction actually live in holes underground.[1]

F. The Destruction of the Market

In forming a judgment as to the economic situation one fact must never be forgotten. The problem which was regarded by the non-party experts once with the Gosplan as being of decisive significance and whose importance was at last recognised even by Stalin in his speech of June 23rd, 1931, has not been solved; this was the problem of preserving the balance of supply and demand on the market, the problem of combining a planned economy with a formally free market. The equilibrium had been disturbed even before the Five Year Plan came into force; it was for this reason that the non-party experts thought the time inopportune for the introduction of the plan. And indeed, currency and market were finally broken up under its operation.

The unfavourable economic situation of Russia is not to be regarded as exclusively the outcome of a failure in production. Equal quantities of consumption goods may satisfy the community's needs in very different degrees, and equal quantities of production goods may bring about very different degrees of expansion in production. It all depends upon the methods of distribution.

The Soviet Russian planned economy consists first of a general expropriation of goods and secondly of a general distribution of goods. The expropriation of

[1] *Za industrializaciu*, August 14, 1933.

goods is a very questionable method from the economic point of view. The famine of 1932 and 1933 was caused not only by the bad harvests, but also, to a considerable extent, by the system of expropriation. The grain harvest of 1924 was, after that of 1921, the least satisfactory; it was worse than the harvest of 1931.[1] Yet in 1924–5 there was no famine over wide areas and although the revival of agriculture was retarded it was not definitely suspended; on the other hand, in 1931 the harvest failure led to severe famine over wide areas and to the decline of agriculture. This difference is explained by the fact that in 1924–5 the Russian Government had to come to terms with agriculture on the market, and although the position of the state buying organisations on the market was powerful it was not one of monopoly. In 1924–5 the Soviet Government could not achieve its purpose, which was to buy so much grain that an export could be effected; in fact, it was compelled to import a certain amount of grain for the large towns, and this procedure was quite in harmony with the real economic interests of the community. In 1931–2, on the other hand, the government was able, thanks to the excellence of its coercive apparatus, to enforce the greatest of all levies and to effect a considerable export. For Russian agriculture the results were catastrophic.

If the expropriation of goods is thus a dangerous instrument in the hands of the government, distribution by authority is an inefficient instrument. Even the

[1] According to the Birmingham Bureau, Memorandum 8, table III, the distribution of the net yield of grain worked out at 2·9 dz. per head of the population in 1924–5, and at 3·5 dz. per head—that is, 20 per cent more—in 1931–2.

distribution of consumption goods which satisfy the most elementary requirements of the population—as, for example, bread—is no simple matter, but requires an extremely complex and very extensive organisation. The authoritative distribution of goods of the second order which satisfy individualised requirements always results in their losing value. Life with rations, food cards and queues is unworthy of the human race.

The fact that Russian industry was concentrated in huge undertakings might lead us to suppose that distribution by authority would be successful, at any rate in the sphere of production goods. But we have already shown what insuperable difficulties were met with here. Even for the distribution of production goods the mechanism of the market was still an incomparably more perfect instrument than the planned economy.

The fact that it was not possible in Soviet Russia to combine a planned economy with a system of market trading is not to be explained simply by the fact that the plans were overstrained. The latter circumstance did indeed bring about a necessary extension of the use of the methods of the "force" economy, but, as we have shown, the collapse of market trading had set in even before the Five Year Plan had come into force—at a time that is when the plans, thanks to the non-party experts, were not worked out without a certain amount of foresight. Russian economic life recovered comparatively quickly only as long as the N.E.P. system functioned properly. But when it did, a consistent planned economy hardly existed. The Soviet Government allowed private trade to cut across its plans. The latter were corrected by the market and the government did not dare to get rid of private business. This correction of planned interference by the elemental forces of the market benefited economic life.

G. The Problem of Unemployment

The most important argument adduced in favour of the Soviet Russian planned economy is this : At a time of world crisis, when in capitalistic countries millions are without work the Soviet Government has succeeded in overcoming unemployment.

Owing to the great difference of structure between the Russian economic system and that of the western capitalistic countries, it is necessary to regard the problem of unemployment in Russia from quite a different point of view. In Russia there is very little connection between unemployment and cyclical fluctuations of industry. The supply of skilled labour in Russia was always scarce and trained workers seldom remained without employment. The roots of Russian unemployment lie not in the cities but in the heavily over-populated rural areas.[1] The latter areas have more than sufficient labour and can hardly feed the entire rural population. When there are prospects of obtaining work in the cities great numbers of peasants stream into them. They satisfy the labour market and create in addition a reserve army of unemployed who wait for some fortunate chance of obtaining work. On the other hand, when there is an industrial crisis the peasants return to the country ; and not only the peasants but also a considerable percentage of the workers who have not yet broken off

[1] There is an admirable analysis of this question in Dr. Michael Hoffmann's *Die agrarische Überbevölkerung Russlands*, Berlin Mannheim-Verlag, 1932, pp. 64–8, 83–4.

their connections with the villages. Thus in Russia we may observe a paradoxical phenomenon—the increase of unemployment under favourable trading conditions in industry and a decline of unemployment with unfavourable conditions. This shows that in Russia the unemployment conditions in the towns provide no useful criterion in estimating the value of an economic policy. Agrarian over-population forms the most delicate problem of Russian economic life, and a Russian economic policy must always be judged by whether it eases agricultural over-population or accentuates it.

The operation of the laws we have mentioned was very clearly in evidence after the revolution. In the years of "War-communism", when industry was in a catastrophic condition, there were no unemployed in the cities, and even by the severest methods of compulsion the Soviet Government was only able to keep a bare third of the workers in their places. They gravitated towards the villages, where at that time all hoped to obtain a portion of land. However unfavourable was the situation in the country, it was more easily possible to survive the crisis there than in the towns.

With the introduction of the new economic policy a process of recovery set in throughout the economic system; the number of industrial workers grew rapidly and their economic situation was actually better in 1926–7 than before the war. A wide gap developed between the conditions of the workers and of the peasants; it is true that the Agrarian revolution had given to the peasants a certain amount of additional land, but on the other hand they were at a much greater disadvantage on the market than they were before the war. The peasants flowed into the towns and the result was that the revival of industry did not lead to the disappearance but rather to an increase in the number of unemployed. The maximum of 1,958 thousand was reached in 1927–8, the last year before the Five Year Plan came into force; the number of unemployed was then not much less than the number of workers in large-scale industry, which amounted to 2,080 thousand.[1] It would be a mistake to condemn on this account the economic policy of the N.E.P. period. At this time economic life recovered rapidly and no catastrophic events occurred.

With the introduction of the Five Year Plan the demand for labour increased very rapidly, but at the same time there was a worsening of food and housing conditions in the towns. In 1928–9, for the first time since the announcement of the New Economic Policy, there was a decrease of unemployment, and after the first campaign to bring about compulsory collectivisation an entirely new situation developed in the spring of 1930 on the labour market; there was a scarcity of labour. This reversal can only be partly explained by the enormous increase in the demand for labour—for the over-populated rural areas of Russia might have met the greatest possible call for workers. The decisive factor was the deterioration of the position of the industrial employees. Once again the towns lost, to a certain extent, their power to attract, just as they lost it under War-communism. Another fact was of great significance; the poor peasants, who had formerly drifted into the towns, now entered the collectives where at first they felt themselves secure. The Soviet Government had to take coercive measures. It compelled the collectives to supply a definite number of workers; it

[1] Control-figures for the year 1928–9, pp. 159, 468.

abolished unemployment benefit and created armies of forced labourers out of the expropriated peasants and political suspects.

The shortage of labour was felt in 1930 and 1931. In 1932 there was again a change in the conditions of the labour market. The great levies plunged the rural population into famine. " In 1932," writes the German agricultural expert Dr. Otto Schiller,[1] " *a considerable percentage of the population was in continual movement* (Schiller's italics) and this was a heavy burden not only on the transport system but also on national production . . . whole villages were deserted. . . ." Railway trains were packed with wandering peasants, and innumerable multitudes, waiting in vain for tickets, besieged the stations. However great was the demand for labour the economic system was unable to make use of these enormous masses of raw workers, especially as the Soviet Government had begun to slow down building activity in the autumn of 1931. The unemployment benefit which had been abolished in the autumn of 1930 had not been revived and the government sought to free itself from the pressing crowds of peasants. The object of the passport law was to keep the peasants from the towns. It was much more convenient to let them starve in the country.

These facts confirm our theory that the development of unemployment is hardly of significance in forming a judgment about Russian economic policy. But of rural over-population, in the conditions ruling in agriculture to-day, it may be said that the situation has taken on a catastrophic character.

Yet there remains the remarkable fact that in a short

[1] *Die Krise der sozialisierten Landwirtschaft in der Sowietunion*, p. 45.

time the number of Russian workers has been doubled. This has been made possible by the fact that the standard of living of the workers was reduced to the lowest level —a level much lower than that of those in receipt of unemployment benefit in capitalist countries. A process such as this can be accomplished by a communist, but hardly by a bourgeois government. Even under the pressure of the world crisis the bourgeois governments did not dare to compel the unemployed to work for low wages. They sought to support the unemployed out of their abundant reserves without cutting down wages. And only when the reserves were exhausted was the system of planned relief works instituted here and there. Under this system the wages of the workers were modest enough but still much better than the normal wages under the Soviet Russian planned economy.

H. Planned Economy as an Economic System for the Future

Since it has become clear that the Five Year Plan has not raised the standard of living of the masses but has rather depressed it, Soviet Russian planned economy is frequently defended in another way. The system, it is said, lowers the condition of the people in the present, but it secures for them a greater degree of prosperity in the future. "The Russian people," says a German economic politician, "has all the qualities to starve itself through to greatness." It should be noted here that such an interpretation of the Soviet Russian planned economy does not represent the intentions of the authors of the Five Year Plan; the latter expected that the condition of the people would at once begin to improve and, what is more, at a rapid rate. Only in the second year of the Five Year period when it became clear that the condition of the masses was deteriorating was a new theory propounded; this said that it was necessary first of all to suffer and that it would pay to make still greater efforts in order, so to speak, to shorten the journey through Purgatory (four years instead of five). The reward would come after the completion of the Five Year Plan; then at one stroke the masses would achieve a much higher standard of living. As the economic situation did not improve after the end of the Five Year period in spite of all "successes" it was realised that socialism had still not been brought to completion and that great efforts would have to be made for yet another five years.

It is not a specific characteristic of the Soviet Russian planned economy that economic life under this system is founded upon a postponement of the satisfaction of certain immediate needs in order to secure the future. But in any system an intelligent relation should exist between the efforts which are made for the present and those made for the future. In an economic system which operates spontaneously, it is true to say that present goods are valued higher than future goods. In harmony with this law there exists an intelligent relation between work for the present and work for the future. A specific feature of the Soviet Russian planned economy is its unbalanced emphasis upon the future, and this in no sense is to be regarded as a virtue. To sacrifice the interests of an entire generation for the sake of the future cannot possibly be justified from an economic point of view.

It is fundamentally mistaken to suppose that the

economic future of a people is served by an entire neglect of its immediate wants. The future is made secure not so much by saving as by hard work in the present. And only a people whose needs are reasonably well satisfied is able to work hard. In Soviet Russia this principle is systematically violated. In 1931–2 a considerable export of grain was effected in order to acquire machinery for the factories then under construction. Yet it is hardly to be doubted that the injury done to agriculture by this export will not be made good in the future by the profits gained from these new factories. The rapid construction of the great power station on the Dnieper rapids (Dneprogez) is accounted one of the most brilliant feats of the Soviet Government, and it has already won for the government the support of many foreign travellers. But from an economic point of view the rapid construction of Dneprogez cannot be justified at all, because many years must elapse before the factories which it is supposed to serve will be completed; there seems, indeed, to be no urgent need for them. Meanwhile no funds are available for house-building in Magnitogorsk, and it is very probable that the unsatisfactory results yielded by this smelting works are the direct outcome of the disgusting conditions in which the workers are compelled to live.

The theory that the Soviet Russian planned economy is a system for the future rests upon another very doubtful premiss. It is supposed that all the buildings and factories which are being built in accordance with the plan will one day be of use to the community. This view is true of many of the buildings, but by no means of all; for the building work is not governed by the principle of profitability, and this principle has, as we have shown, an absolute value in economics. It is not only probable that many of the factories will fail to yield any return on the capital invested in them (and this means that the capital could more usefully have been invested in other undertakings), it is even probable that their receipts will not cover their running expenses. Such doubts are awakened particularly by the Soviet Government's greatest projects, the enterprises in which it takes the greatest pride. For reasons which have already been mentioned the profitability of the Magnitogorsk-Kuzneck combine is very questionable. The production of very complex machinery in Russia is doubtful from the point of view of profitability ; it is much too expensive and the work is often of low quality.

These undertakings have been attempted with the energy which is characteristic of a revolutionary epoch, and something positive will even yet crystallise out of them. But there can be no question of justifying, from an economic point of view, the enormous sacrifice called for by such an experiment. On the eve of the World War, Russian industry was making great progress, and this progress demanded no sacrifice from the people.

At any rate, under a planned economy with shattered markets it is impossible to make a proper choice between factories which it pays to use and factories which it does not pay to use. Only within the framework of a market economy are the prices of consumption goods formed in such a way that they correctly express the comparative urgency of demand ; only within the framework of a market economy are the prices of production goods correctly formed by the method of imputation. Rational selection in the use of plant constructed under a planned economy can only be achieved under a market economy.

ECONOMIC PLANNING IN SOVIET RUSSIA

I. The Extra-Economic Basis of the Soviet Russian Planned Economy

At the end of 1932 the masses were so badly fed and the condition of the collectives, the state farms and of industry was so unfavourable that Stalin, who least of all lacks confidence, did not dare to justify the Five Year Plan on purely economic grounds. In his speech of January 7th, 1933, where he summed up the results of the plan, he laid great emphasis upon its extra-economic basis. He had to admit that economic life might be allowed to develop in another direction and that this would lead to a greater satisfaction of the people's needs: "But in this case," he said, "we should not have at our disposal all the modern means of defence, without which the national independence of a country is impossible, without which the country is transformed into an object of attack by external enemies." In addition he called particular attention to two further non-economic aims: to make the country economically independent of the capitalist world (autarchy) and to overcome the capitalist elements in the country. Communist writers find it particularly difficult to prove that agriculture is making progress; they content themselves with showing that it has been possible to socialise agriculture, and to gather it into great enterprises, pointing out that this has been done much more quickly than the Five Year Plan specified. They would like to identify agricultural socialisation with agricultural progress.

It must be admitted that communism cannot be assailed in this position. If the problem consists of making the economic system serve extra-economic ends then the planned economy provides an excellent solution.

Of that, indeed, even the capitalist world seems to have been clear. When the capitalist countries wished to gather up all their strength with a view to prosecuting war they found themselves compelled to remodel the economic system on the lines of a planned economy with certain communistic characteristics. But for the western countries this was only a passing phase; at the end of the war such "etatism" was condemned and abolished. Russian communism must be regarded as an attempt to develop the war economy and to give it a new direction and purpose.

An inner union between economics and politics is the essence of the Soviet Russian planned economy. Every economic policy is to a certain extent politics; that is to say one of its aims is to support and strengthen the existing political organisation by economic measures. Yet every capitalist government—if we ignore such quite exceptional and passing events as a world war—acts in this sphere within fairly narrow limits. A bourgeois government does not carry on economic activities and for this reason it must always reckon with the legal independence of the economic system. The interests of the nobility lay nearest to the Russian autocratic government of the pre-1905 period. It spared no pains to secure the landed estates of the nobles and to support their agriculture. And yet it was compelled somehow or other to accommodate itself to the gradual and economically inevitable reduction of these landed estates—a process which implied the breakdown of the government's social foundation. The government felt that the development of industrial capitalism created difficulties which it would find extraordinarily difficult to overcome. Nevertheless, it was compelled for economic reasons not only to tolerate the development of capitalist large-scale industry but even to favour it. The spontaneous development of the economic system imposed restrictions upon the Tsarist Government from which it was not in a position to free itself.

With the victory of the planned economy, economic life was finally subordinated to politics, for under this system the government itself carries on economic activities and does not permit the people to do so. Only under a planned economy is it possible for a government to undertake the task of abolishing the age-old organisation of agriculture and of replacing it at a stroke by another organisation, the nature of which it is only able to imagine in its most general outline. Every government may make mistakes in its economic policy ; but only the planned economy bestows upon the government so much power that such mistakes may develop into catastrophes and yet hardly endanger the position of the government. For a government which is all-powerful economically is also all-powerful politically.

The character of the political ideals which a communist government seeks to impose upon the economic system is determined by the nature and history of the government in question. A party which has survived so great a conflict could only achieve victory by virtue of fanatical faith ; by virtue of the belief that, as bearer of the pure socialist doctrine, it was the final flower of the social and spiritual evolution of European civilisation ; that it was called upon to deliver all mankind. It is natural for such a party to identify the good of the masses with the good of the " government of the proletarian dictatorship ". That socialism will bring happiness to all mankind is a proposition about which such a party can have not even a suspicion of doubt. And if this be the case, of what significance are the passing sufferings of the people, of what significance is the ruin of a few million peasants—compared to the immortal political interests of the government of the world revolution ?

In such a planned economy the character of the economic administration, not only of the central authorities, but also of every tiny branch, must be political ; everywhere the interests of those engaged in economic activities must be subordinated to the interests of the all-embracing socialist state. At the head of every enterprise, however modest, there must stand a politically trustworthy man—a communist. Under the communist planned economy the economic system is managed not by experts but by laymen ; and that is one important reason for the failure of the system.[1]

[1] If we required any confirmation of our estimate of the Soviet Russian economic plan, we should be justified in appealing to the opinion of the intelligentsia, whose past records show that they have ever been devoted to the interests of the suffering masses of the people. When the Soviet Government announced the N.E.P., the intelligentsia went into harness to drag Russian economy out of the bog into which that same government had thrown it. They believed that they could thus serve their people best and they renounced all political ambitions. Their relations with the communists were at that time satisfactory. But after the breakdown of the N.E.P. system, it became increasingly difficult for them to work with the Soviet Government, and after the Right wing of the party had been routed in the year 1930, there set in a frightful period of persecution of the intellectuals. They were thrown into prison wholesale or sent to concentration camps, and not a few of them were shot outright. All the prominent economists, such as Kondratiev, Wainstein, Tschajanow, Makarov, Oganovsky, Groman, Bazarov and Ginzburg, fell victims to this persecution, which may be attributed partly to the government's need of a scapegoat to pacify the people, but partly, also, to the fact that the intellectuals could not possibly give their approval to the government's economic policy of those days. If we ignore for the moment the self-accusations wrung

The starting-point of the socialist's criticism of the capitalist system is the complaint that the latter is not concerned first of all to supply the needs of the population. Socialism claims, on the other hand, to provide such a system. Now in the Soviet Russian planned economy we have an economic system which is conceived entirely from a political point of view ; and this system has entirely subordinated the satisfying of the needs of the population. This political degeneration of an economic system shows how dangerous is any attempt to eliminate finally the controlling forces of the market from the economic life of a people. There is no evidence to show that the socialist economic plan, even when based on a money system, is able to meet the requirements of the masses in a normal way. On the other hand, there is evidence that such a system can, more easily than any other, be misused to achieve non-economic aims while shelving entirely the problem of maintaining the nation's supplies.

from the morally or physically tortured intellectuals at their public trials, we can see that there is some truth in the complaints that were made against them. They were undeniably hostile to the existing system, which was purely political in its tendencies. They could not possibly connive at such cruel measures as the raising of monstrous levies, the enforced collectivity, the " Dekulakisation " and others. They endeavoured to put a brake on these activities, relying for support on the Right wing's disaffection. But in the communist state every dissenting opinion is branded as sabotage and hunted down. This negative attitude of the Russian intellectuals towards the Soviet economic system, which has cost them innumerable victims, carries far more weight than the optimistic accounts brought home by foreign travellers, who have no knowledge of the country or the language, are conducted everywhere by communists and proceed to describe in their impressions just what they have been told by their guides.

For Product Safety Concerns and Information please contact our EU representative GPSR@taylorandfrancis.com
Taylor & Francis Verlag GmbH, Kaufingerstraße 24, 80331 München, Germany

www.ingramcontent.com/pod-product-compliance
Lightning Source LLC
LaVergne TN
LVHW011123300926
849160LV00008B/498

* 9 7 8 1 1 3 8 5 6 6 0 8 8 *